Big
Business
Economic Power in a Free Society

Big
Business
Economic Power in a Free Society

Advisory Editor
LEON STEIN

Editorial Board
Stuart Bruchey
Thomas C. Cochran

A NOTE ABOUT THIS BOOK

Gilbert H. Montague was Ricardo Scholar of Economics at Harvard University. In this book, he offers a careful review of the origin and extent of the economic power wielded by the Standard Oil Company, giving special attention to the rebate arrangements and manipulations involving the makers and operators of pipelines. In writing about this complex story, a *New York Times* reviewer said, "the author is most careful not to exaggerate any of the conditions, past or present, nor is he ever personal in his criticisms, and he is too wise to indulge in any prophesies."

THE RISE AND PROGRESS
OF THE
STANDARD OIL COMPANY

BY

GILBERT HOLLAND MONTAGUE

WITHDRAWN

ARNO PRESS

A New York Times Company

New York / 1973

250411

Reprint Edition 1973 by Arno Press Inc.

Reprinted from a copy in
The University of Illinois Library

BIG BUSINESS: Economic Power in a Free Society
ISBN for complete set: 0-405-05070-4
See last pages of this volume for titles.

Manufactured in the United States of America

Library of Congress Cataloging in Publication Data

Montague, Gilbert Holland, 1880-1961.
    The rise and progress of the Standard Oil Company.

    (Big business: economic power in a free society)
    Reprint of the ed. published by Harper, New York.
    1. Standard Oil Company. I. Title. II. Series.
HD2769.O4M8   1973   338.7'66'550973   73-2525
ISBN 0-405-05104-2

THE RISE AND PROGRESS
OF THE
STANDARD OIL COMPANY

BY

GILBERT HOLLAND MONTAGUE

NEW YORK AND LONDON
HARPER & BROTHERS
PUBLISHERS ❧ MCMIV

PREFACE

THE study of the Standard Oil Company—
of which this book is the outcome—was
undertaken by the author while Ricardo
Scholar in Economics at Harvard University for the year 1900–1901. The results
of this study were reported from time to
time to the Seminary of the Department
of Economics, and eventually were printed
in the *Quarterly Journal of Economics* published for Harvard University. The period from 1865 till 1879 was treated in the
Quarterly for February, 1902, in an article
entitled " The Rise and Supremacy of the
Standard Oil Company "; and in the *Quarterly* for February, 1903, under the title of
" The Later History of the Standard Oil
Company," the narrative was continued to

the present. By the courtesy of the editors and the publishers of the *Quarterly Journal of Economics* these two articles, which together compose this book, are reprinted unchanged.

The sources of this history are the reports of official investigating commissions and committees. Chief of these are the report of the "Hepburn" committee appointed in 1879 by the Legislature of New York to investigate railway abuses; the report submitted to Congress in 1888 by the committee appointed to investigate trusts, and the report of the Industrial Commission appointed by the President in 1898 and making its preliminary report on trusts in 1900.

The oil business, in its early phase, was the reflex of prevalent railway methods. To attempt to judge the situation without first ascertaining the standards set by the railway management of the time is not merely unfair, it is subversive of all historical accuracy. The South Improve-

ment Company of 1872 is an instance in
point. Its interrupted contracts with the
railroads have since been generally exe-
crated, and, as it is shown in these pages,
probably rightly. But, while condemning
these contracts, be it remembered that
they followed in principle the best lights
of the railway economy of the period; that
they were part of the generally accepted
"evening system," by which railways in
perfect good faith protected themselves
against disastrous competition. To ap-
point a group of the largest shippers
"eveners," and in return for a special
rebate require them to apportion traffic
among the roads, seemed at that time a
practice both inevitable and legitimate.
This knowledge of contemporary railroad
history may not change the current judgment upon the contracts of the South
Improvement Company; but it helps to a
fairer distribution of the blame, if there
be any, between the railroads and the
company.

Preface

The constant reference in the text to authorities in the foot-notes will not, it is hoped, detract from the narrative. In a matter so much discussed as the subject of this history there seems no longer room for unverified opinion. And if verification seems sometimes too insistent, the importance of authenticating facts which too often have been loosely disputed should be sufficient excuse.

GILBERT HOLLAND MONTAGUE.

CAMBRIDGE, MASSACHUSETTS.

THE RISE AND PROGRESS

OF THE

STANDARD OIL COMPANY

THE RISE AND PROGRESS

OF THE

STANDARD OIL COMPANY

I

THE rise and progress of the Standard
Oil Company, from its inception in 1865
till its control, in 1878, of ninety - five
per cent. of the oil business of the United
States, has presented itself to different
critics in somewhat different characters;
certain conservative writers think it was
largely the result of discriminations in
freight rates, extorted by more or less
questionable practices from the easy virtue
of the railroads. But just why the railroads found it expedient to grant such
unusual favors, and why this particular

group of men, above all others, proved best able to extort such favors, no one has satisfactorily explained. Corruption of the railway officials has been vaguely suggested; but it has not been shown whence this group of men had the means to suborn the railways, and no writer has been able to point to a piece of precise evidence, found by any court or investigating committee in the United States, which proved such subornation of railway officials, though it is not inconceivable that some evidence may exist. Congressional and legislative committees, on the other hand, and the more cautious writers on trusts, have been equally put to it to find in those acts of the railways which eventually made the Standard Oil Company supreme any self-interested motives. The fact of the discrimination in freight rates seems to account for the supremacy of the Standard Oil Company. But why those refiners identified with the Standard Oil Company, instead of

2

some other group of refiners, should persistently have obtained the best rates, has been, to these investigators, a baffling mystery.

The secret of this strange success with the railways is not, however, completely insoluble. If the episodes in the progress of the Standard Oil Company from 1865 till 1877 be carefully studied, the motives of every act, both of the company and of the railways, will certainly be revealed. The materials for this study are not lacking. A vast amount of evidence showing the ability of the Standard Oil Company to turn these possibilities to advantage has been gathered by various commissions and investigating committees. With such sources of information as these available, an intelligible narrative may readily be put together. Not only may each act of the company and of the railways be authenticated, but also, at each step in the progress, the increasing efficiency and importance of the

3

company may be estimated, and the momentary opportunities of railway and industrial conditions may be gauged. And so in what seems at first sight an unaccountable and suspiciously rapid growth may be discerned signs of inevitable development—the operation of motives which are, at any rate, explicable.

1865–70

In 1865, when Mr. John D. Rockefeller began in a small way to refine petroleum at Cleveland, Ohio, the oil industry was in a singularly inchoate state. With the success of Drake's oil-well at Titusville, Pennsylvania, in 1859, refiners had been released from the necessity of distilling coal into petroleum before refining petroleum into kerosene; and at the same time the sources of petroleum were shown to be enormously greater than they had ever before been guessed. This discovery stimulated consumers to increased use of lubri-

4

cants and burning oils, and in this way
rapidly increased the demand in the arts
for the refined product. In even greater
measure it encouraged the production of
crude petroleum. Within a year after
Drake's success wells had been sunk all
around Oil City and along the Alleghany
River. In 1864 had occurred the Cherry
"run," followed by the Benninghoff and
the Pioneer "runs" and the sensational
exploitation of Pithole Creek. While Mr.
Rockefeller was erecting his little refinery,
Pithole City—now a field sown with wheat
—had a post-office nearly as large as that
of Philadelphia. From Manitoulin Island
to Alabama, and from Missouri to Central
New York, wells had been bored for oil.
So rapid had been the increased demand
for the products of petroleum, and so unexpected had been the increase of supply,
that in 1865 existing refineries proved
quite inadequate to the business suddenly
thrust upon them.

The difficulties besetting refiners in 1865

were chiefly such as could be cured by an increase of capital. In 1861 the best wells had been thirty miles from the railroads. Because of the lack of barrels and the difficulty of transportation, petroleum had fallen from $20 a barrel to almost nothing. By 1863 boats had begun transporting petroleum down Oil Creek, and small pipelines and branch railway lines had been built. In 1866 a more efficient cylinder refining-still was invented, casing and torpedoes were coming to be used in drilling, the tank-car began to replace the clumsy flat-car with its wooden tubs, and pipe-lines regularly transported petroleum from the wells to the railroads. To secure these economies in refining, small concerns must either increase their capital to about $500,000 or else combine into this larger and more efficient unit of production. Mr. Rockefeller was among the first to see the exigency; and in 1867 he united into the firm of Rockefeller, Andrews & Flagler the refineries of William Rockefeller &

Co., Rockefeller & Andrews, Rockefeller &
Co., S. V. Harkness, and H. M. Flagler.
The reasons for this union, as he afterwards stated them, must even then have
been evident: "The cause leading to the
combination was the desire to unite our
skill and capital, in order to carry on a
business of some magnitude and importance in place of the small business that
each had separately heretofore carried
on."[1]

With the reorganization of the firm of
Rockefeller, Andrews & Flagler, in 1870,
into the Standard Oil Company of Ohio,
with capital stock of $1,000,000, the first
period of the oil industry may be said to
close. No company had sought, or, indeed, has since sought, to control the oil-
fields. So far as may be known, no refiner
had yet organized the pipe-lines to his exclusive advantage or exacted of the railroads better freight rates than were grant-

[1] *Report of the Industrial Commission*, 1900, p.
799.

7

ed to his competitor. The transportation of oil by rail and by pipe-line was left to independent companies, and it was only by the competition and by the improvements of such companies that the cost of the transportation had been reduced. Till 1870 the competition of refiners was solely concerned with efficiency of production; and, since this was to be gained only by refineries of $500,000 capitalization or more, there was concentration among the stronger concerns and extermination of the weaker. By its process of concentration, and solely on account of its superior efficiency, the Standard Oil Company of Ohio became in 1870 larger than most of its competitors, and produced four per cent. of all the oil refined.[1] After 1870 the progress of the

[1] Evidence as to the capacity of the Standard Oil Company of Ohio in 1870. — B. B. Campbell (a prominent opponent of the Standard Oil Company) (*Investigation of Trusts*, Congress, 1888, p. 116):
"*Question.* How large at that time [1870] was the

oil industry, generally, and the precedence
of the Standard Oil Company, in particular, was to lie in the direction of cheaper
transportation exacted of the transportation companies by the refiners.

interest of those who now represent the Standard
Oil Trust?

"*Answer.* Not *much* larger interest, I should
judge, than some of their competitors."

Charles T. Morehouse ("*Hepburn*" *Report*, New
York, 1879, p. 2624):

"*Q.* Now tell us what was their [the Standard Oil
Company's] capacity then [1870] as compared with
other works at Cleveland and other points?

"*A.* Not as large as some of the other works, . . .
but comparing very favorably with such works as
Charles Pratt & Co. and three or four in the oil
regions."

Lewis Emery (at present the most prominent opponent of the Standard Oil Company) (*Report of the
Industrial Commission*, 1900, p. 646):

"Mr. H. M. Flagler swore they had a capacity of
six hundred barrels per day of crude oil in their refinery, the production at that time [1870] being
about sixteen thousand barrels a day. That would
give them four per cent. of the refining business at
that time. At that time there existed in the oil
country, spread from Louisville, Kentucky, to Port-
land, Maine, more than two hundred and fifty refineries."

1870–74

Though the progress of the oil industry from 1865 till 1870 be said to have determined the most efficient unit of production, and though the advance of the next seven years be said to consist in cheapening the transportation of oil, yet it must not be forgotten that a considerable advance in refining took place in this later period. Large refineries soon began manufacturing for their own use barrels, tin cans, boxes for enclosing cans, paint, glue, and sulphuric acid. By experiment the process of distillation was made applicable to qualities of petroleum which previously had been almost useless. By improvement in the details of refining, more durable machinery, tanks, and pumps were constructed, and a better illuminant was produced at less cost. In 1875 a method had been devised of utilizing the residuum of crude petroleum left after the manufacture of illuminating oil; and, after the

example of the shale works of Scotland,
the process of refining lubricants and paraffine wax from the waste that previously
was used as fuel had been adopted in the
larger refineries. These improvements,
however, were by no means so considerable
in the period from 1870 till 1877 as the advantage from the control of transportation; and, though they rendered unprofitable those refineries which could not buy
better machinery or utilize their residuum,
they were quite too generally adopted by
large refiners to account for the growing
pre-eminence of the Standard Oil Company.

From 1870 till 1877, then, the struggle of
the refiners was chiefly for transportation
facilities. Until the issuance of the so-
called "Rutter Circular," in 1874, the advantage they sought lay chiefly in discriminating freight rates. From 1874 till
1877 the large refiners sought both to obtain special rates from the railroads and to
organize into systems for their own ad-

vantage the bewildering net-work of pipe-lines that had been building since 1869. By surpassing skill in both regions of activity the Standard Oil Company grew in seven years from a concern controlling four per cent. of the refined oil output into one controlling ninety-five per cent. Organization of the pipe-lines came late, because of the excessive amount of capital it demanded. Opportunities for discriminating freight rates, however, presented themselves early. How the Standard Oil Company availed itself of the unique railway conditions and of the practices common in the freight traffic of that time is one of the most sensational episodes in the history of American railroads.

By 1871 the New York Central, the Erie, and the Pennsylvania railroads had completed connections that afforded them entrance to Chicago, and the great struggle for the traffic of the West had set in. The roads were so poor, and the necessity for revenue so great, that rate wars had begun

THE STANDARD OIL COMPANY

as early as 1869, when the New York Central and the Pennsylvania roads had secured connection with Chicago. With the entrance of the Erie road and, in 1874, of the Baltimore and Ohio into Chicago, the competition for traffic throughout the region of the trunk lines became more embittered. During the years from 1869 till 1873 the agents of the roads met annually at New York to agree upon freight rates; and afterwards, in order to get traffic, they regularly broke their agreement. Every year during this period fourth-class rates from Chicago to New York fell from about 80 cents per one hundred pounds in December to about 25 cents in August and September. This reckless competition for traffic was extended to the oil regions. The Pennsylvania Railroad, which had the earliest and closest connection with the centre of petroleum production at Oil City, hauled oil to Pittsburg, a distance of eighty miles, and to Philadelphia, a distance of four hundred miles.

13

The Erie Railroad, which had no direct communication with the oil country, effected an entrance by a connection with the Atlantic and Great Western road, and hauled oil from Oil City to New York, a distance of five hundred and fifty miles. The New York Central Railroad entered Oil City by connections at Cleveland, and hauled oil to New York, a distance of seven hundred and forty miles. Just as agents of the roads had annually agreed upon a rate from Chicago to the seaboard, making the charge 80 cents by each road with a differential of 5 cents in favor of Baltimore and Philadelphia, so in the case of the oil traffic the same rate was charged by each road on oil moving from Oil City to the seaboard. The effect of this "group rate" was naturally displeasing to refiners at Pittsburg: it deprived them of all geographical advantage, and enabled their competitors at Cleveland—among others, the Standard Oil Company—to ship oil seven hundred and forty miles by the New

York Central Railroad at precisely the
rate they were charged for a haulage of
four hundred miles.

Clearly this was a coincidence in
rates not based upon any correspond-
ing coincidence of cost, and as such
constituted a case of discrimination. The
competition of the railroads, however,
was so fierce as to make no other adjustment practicable. In the practice
and theory of railway rates, moreover,
ample economic justification is to be
found.

Because of the futility of basing rates on
cost of service, a system of freight rates
has arisen which favors certain classes of
goods, certain localities, and certain individuals. By lowering rates on cheap
goods, by lowering rates at competitive
points, and by lowering rates to benefit growing concerns, the revenue of the
railways is greatly increased with very
slight increase in its expenses. By lowering rates in those three ways, then, and

charging "what the traffic will bear," the railways may do business most cheaply, give lowest rates, and make the most profit. In pursuance of this principle, discriminations of the first sort have been practised from the earliest times. "Group rates"—a form of the second sort of discrimination—have been freely made since 1869, when the railways first made the rates uniform on all the routes between the competitive points of New York and Chicago. Similar "group rates" have since been established in the coal traffic from the anthracite regions to the seaboard, and in the fruit traffic of California and Florida. The prominence of such "group rates" in the pooling agreements of the trunk lines in 1873, 1875, and 1877, and in the "Southwestern pooling agreements" of 1879, show how general was their acceptance. So fundamental, indeed, have they become in American railway tariffs that the Interstate Commerce Commission has repeatedly sanctioned them.[1] Discriminations of the third sort were common throughout the period from 1870 till 1874, and by 1875 the "evening system"—a form of the third class of discriminations which the South Improvement Company closely anticipated—had become especially prominent in the cattle business between New York and Chicago.[2] These

[1] In the milk cases (*Report of the Interstate Commerce Commission*, ii., p. 273; vii., p. 97) the principle of the " group rates " is interestingly discussed from the most conservative stand-point.

[2] The principle of the "cattle eveners' agreement" has been stated as follows: "The trunk lines leading to New York agreed upon a per cent. of the business which each road should receive, and appointed three cattle eveners, whose duty it was to see that the shipments were made over all the roads in the agreed proportions; and for that service they were to receive $15 a car . . . on every car-load of cattle shipped from the West to New York, no matter by whom shipped. . . . The commission was later reduced to $10. Now every man is made his own evener—*i.e.*, if he ships his cattle by the road he is requested to he gets a certain price; if he ships contrary to directions his price is made $10 higher; and this is said to work very well, the rates *via* all routes of course being the same."—*Report of the "Hepburn" Committee*, New York, 1879, pp. 69, 70.

17

various sorts of discrimination, then—
special tariffs, "group rates," and "evening systems"—must all be regarded as
practices inevitable in the railway management of the period—as essential con-
sequences of railway economy in its development.

In one way or another every advantage
obtained in rates by the large refiners at
Cleveland, in the period from 1870 till
1874, may be classified under one of these
three sorts of discrimination. As soon as
oil became a prominent export they benefited, with all other refiners, in the special
rates on oil in barrels and in tanks. Under
the "group rates" on oil from Oil City to
the seaboard they enjoyed local discrimination—a discrimination doubtless annoy-
ing to refiners on the shorter routes, but
not essentially different from that of the
"group rate" from Chicago to New York,
or those later enforced by pools and authorized by the Interstate Commerce Commission. And in 1872 they obtained from

the railroads, under the abortive contract of the South Improvement Company, an "evening arrangement" that, whether wrongly or not, has since become a hissing and a by-word with every opponent of the Standard Oil Company.

Early in 1871 the advantage of Cleveland over Pittsburg, as a refining centre, had become evident. Cleveland not only enjoyed the same railroad rates that Pittsburg had, but also had water communication to the East by way of the great lakes and the Erie Canal. Pittsburg depended almost entirely for transportation upon the railroads. Cleveland, however, could at any time avail herself of the competition of rail and water transportation by taking to lake vessels whenever the charges of the New York Central Railroad were unsatisfactory.

Cleveland, as a competitive point, had the oil traffic of the New York Central at her mercy. Unless the refiners at Cleveland were allowed low freight rates, the New York Central must see its traffic directed to lake vessels. As the danger of such loss became more imminent, the New York Central was obliged to grant greater and greater favors to the refiners. And when, in 1871, an unexpected shift in the centre of oil production threatened the entire refining business at Cleveland, the railroads dependent on this business were stirred to unusual action.

Beginning in 1871, at the Clarion River, remarkable discoveries of petroleum had been made throughout Butler and Clarion counties, in the region extending five miles beyond Antwerp, and southwestward a distance of fifteen miles to Millerstown and Greece City. "The development southward," says the editor of the *Oil City Derrick*,[1] "brought about conditions through which some of the most im-

[1] P. C. Boyle, *Report of the Industrial Commission*, 1900, p. 421.

portant railroads of the country might be
deprived of a share of the oil-carrying
trade. The Pennsylvania Railroad, however, was not affected by the transfer of
activities from the Venango region to that
of Butler and Clarion counties. The
northern railway lines—namely, the Erie
and New York Central—were naturally
affected by the transfer of operations to
distant fields, which they could not reach
with their existing connections. The first-
named road was materially aided by the
gathering lines of the Pennsylvania Transportation Company, operated by Henry
Harley; but the New York Central and its
connections were left without petroleum-
feeders of any description." As usual in
new developments of territory, the increase in production due to the large capacity of the wells, the over-capacity of the
pipe-lines in the older oil-fields, and the
over-production of refining plants which
had taken place in the last two years—all
these had conspired to make the transpor-

tation and refining of oil unremuner-
ative throughout the petroleum country, and especially unprofitable at Cleveland.

To remedy this situation, a combination
of the railroads and certain refiners was
planned. "It had its inception," to quote
again the editor of the *Oil City Derrick*,[1]
"with certain Philadelphia and Pittsburg
refiners, with an agreement for co-operation with certain Cleveland refiners. But
philosophical minds, viewing the subject
from this distance, are agreed that it had
its origin, as a matter of fact, with the railroad interests rather than with the oil
interests." The form which this combination took was a contract between the
railroads and certain refiners of Pittsburg, Philadelphia, and Cleveland organ-

---

[1] Boyle, *Report of the Industrial Commission*, 1900,
p. 421. Mr. Boyle's impartiality has been questioned
by opponents of the Standard Oil Company (see
Report of the Industrial Commission, 1900, p. 398),
but has never been disproved.

ized into the South Improvement Company.

By an act of the Pennsylvania Legislature on May 1, 1871, the South Improvement Company had been created and vested with all the powers conferred by the act of April 7, 1870, upon the Pennsylvania Company. The powers of the company included authority "to construct and operate any work or works, public or private, designed to include, increase, facilitate, or develop trade, travel, or the transportation of freight, live-stock, passengers, or any traffic by land or water, from or to any part of the United States." [1] Of the two thousand shares of this company, nine hundred were owned by Messrs. H. M. Flagler, O. H. Payne, William Rockefeller, H. Bostwick, and J. D. Rockefeller, who later were to become prominent in the Standard Oil Company.[2]

[1] *Report of the Industrial Commission*, 1900, p. 607.
[2] Lewis Emery, *Report of the Industrial Commission*, 1900, p. 619.

On January 18, 1872, the South Improvement Company effected the desired combination by completing contracts with the Pennsylvania, the New York Central, and the Erie railroads. According to the contracts[1] the South Improvement Company agreed to ship forty-five per cent. of all the oil transported by it over the Pennsylvania Railroad, and to divide the remainder equally between the Erie and the New York Central railroads, to furnish suitable tankage facilities for shipping petroleum and receiving it at its destination, and to keep records of the amount of petroleum and its products shipped over the railroads both by itself and by other parties. The railroads in return agreed to allow the South Improvement Company rebates on *all* petroleum and its products carried by them, to charge all other parties not less than the full rates specified in the

[1] These contracts are printed in full in "*Hepburn*" *Report*, Exhibits, New York, 1879, pp. 418–449.

contract,[1] to furnish to the South Improvement Company way-bills of all petroleum
or its product transported over their lines
by any parties whatsoever, and, finally,
"at all times to co-operate, as far as it
legally may, with the party hereto of the
first part, to maintain the business of the
party hereto of the first part against loss
or injury by competition, to the end that
the party hereto of the first part may keep

[1] Rates and rebates according to contract:
"ON CRUDE PETROLEUM

	Gross Rate (a).	Rebate (a).
"From any common point to		
Cleveland	$0.80	$0.40
Pittsburg	.80	.40
New York	2.56	1.06

"ON REFINED OIL, ETC.

"From Pittsburg to New York	$2.00	$0.50
"From Cleveland to New York	2.00	.50"

"This contract provided that the railways should
increase the freight to about double what they had
been charging on all oil shipped."—M. L. Lock-
wood, *Report of the Industrial Commission*, 1900,
p. 385.

(a) For each barrel of forty-five gallons. "*Hepburn*" *Report*, Exhibits, New York, 1879, p. 422.

up a remunerative, and so a full and regular business, and to that end shall lower or raise the gross rates of transportation over its railroads and connections, as far as it legally may, for such times and to such extent as may be necessary to overcome such competition." The aim of the railroads, as avowed in the preamble, was plainly an increase in traffic: "whereas the magnitude and extent of the business and operations to be carried on by the party hereto of the first part will greatly promote the interest of the party hereto of the second part, and make it desirable for it by fixing certain rates of freight, drawbacks, and rebates, and by the other provisions of this agreement to encourage the outlay proposed by the party hereto of the first part, and to facilitate and increase the transportation to be received from it, . . . the party hereto of the second part covenants and agrees." And for the attainment of that end, the railroads reserved the right to grant similar rebates and advantages to

26

any other party who should furnish an
amount of transportation equal to that
furnished by the South Improvement
Company, and equal facilities for promot-
ing the petroleum trade.

In general outline the contract was very
like those subsequently made with the
grain-elevator owners in the Northwest,
and with the cattle-shippers of Chicago.
Throughout this period it was the policy
of the railroads to bind to themselves growing businesses, in which, as in the elevator
and refining industries, considerable capital and much enterprise were necessary
in order to succeed, and by granting to
these concerns special rates to build up
trade for the industries and traffic for
themselves. By this form of personal
discrimination the railroads entering New
York had built up traffic for themselves
and business for A. T. Stewart, who was
competing for the market in the Central
West with Field, Leiter & Co., of Chicago.
Where the competition for traffic was keen,

the railroads usually contracted with the strongest shipper or group of shippers to carry freight at a special rate, or else—as in the case of the large cattle-shippers at Chicago and the South Improvement Company in the oil regions — appointed the group "evener," and in return for a special rebate required it to apportion traffic among the roads according to a fixed ratio.[1]

Such are the economic grounds on which to judge this contract. Popular judgment, however, was much less deliberate. On January 18th the contract was signed; and on February 27th, the day after the contract went into effect, an excited mass-meeting was held at Titusville and an organization to oppose the new company hastily effected. At once a complete embargo was placed on the sale of oil to

[1] As to the frequency of such discriminations, see the "*Hepburn*" *Report*, New York, 1879, pp. 48–71. The plan of the cattle-eveners' contract is contained in the "*Hepburn*" *Report*, New York, 1879, p. 70; of A. T. Stewart's contract, "*Hepburn*" *Report*, pp. 452, 808, 1597.

the South Improvement Company. Committees were hurriedly despatched to the railway officials, to Harrisburg, and to Washington. On March 15th a resolution was introduced into the House of Representatives at Washington to investigate the South Improvement Company. On March 25th, in an agreement signed by the independent refiners, the railroads publicly abrogated their contract with the company, and announced that "all arrangements for the transportation of oil after this date shall be upon a basis of perfect equality to all shippers, producers, and refiners, and that no rebates, drawbacks, or other arrangements of any character shall be made or allowed that will give any party the slightest difference in rates or any discrimination of any character whatever;[1] and, with this announcement, they issued new rates about forty per cent. lower than those provided by the contract.

[1] *Investigation of Trusts*, Congress, 1888, p. 361.

On April 6th, before it had the opportunity to do any business, the South Improvement Company was summarily deprived of its charter by the Pennsylvania Legislature. The company has never since had an apologist. The Standard Oil Company, in spite of its part in the unfortunate combination, has always disapproved of the contract.[1] And the bitterest reproach which opponents of the Standard Oil Company heap against it is the taunt that the contract of the South Improvement Company was renewed with the Standard "alliance," which was then forming.[2]

[1] John D. Archbold, *Report of the Industrial Commission*, 1900, p. 540:

"I have no knowledge of any relations on the part of the Standard Oil Company succeeding to the South Improvement Company whatever. I have been an opponent of the South Improvement Company, as you well know. I have disapproved of it in theory, and practically disapproved of it to-day. I want to say that the statements that what was the South Improvement Company is continued in the Standard are not true; if they had been true, I would not have been in it."

[2] Such statements are made by H. D. Lloyd,

THE STANDARD OIL COMPANY

In the condition which led in 1872 to the formation and the contract of the South Improvement Company lies the fact that must decide economic opinion upon the company. Since 1867, competition in refining methods had ruined most of the smaller refineries. By 1869, all but fifteen had for this reason been obliged to sell out to more efficient concerns.[1] In 1869 began the competition between railways that re-

Wealth against Commonwealth, pp. 58–60; J. F. Hudson, *Railways and the Republic*, pp. 70, 71; E. C. Patterson, "*Hepburn*" *Report*, New York, 1879, p. 1693; W. T. Scheide, Ibid., p. 2766; A. B. Hepburn, *Report of the Committee*, Ibid., p. 42; B. B. Campbell, *Investigation of Trusts*, Congress, 1888, p. 364; Lewis Emery, *Report of the Industrial Commission*, 1900, pp. 639–645; George Rice, Ibid., p. 694. No confirming evidence has been offered.

[1] H. H. Rogers ("*Hepburn*" *Report*, New York, 1879, p. 2605):

"*Q.* Was the Standard Oil Company at that time [1872] a large producer? *A.* Oh yes!

"*Q.* Was the Standard Oil Company at that time the largest producer? *A.* The largest refiner, yes.

"*Q.* Where? *A.* In Cleveland and New York, and I think they had some interests in the oil regions."

sulted almost immediately in personal discrimination in rates, and hastened the extermination of such refineries as were already declining. Over-production of oil in 1870 and 1871 had increased the depression, so that in 1872, when the centre of operations was shifted southward, and ruin threatened the large refineries as well as the small, feeling throughout the industry was extremely nervous. According to their usual practice at that time the railways cast about for the strongest group of refiners with whom they might ally to protect their traffic. That the South Improvement Company was the strongest group of refiners has never been disputed. In 1872 the Standard Oil Company was the largest concern in the oil region, and the combined capacity of the refineries organized into the South Improvement Company far exceeded that of the unorganized refiners.[1] That the industrial efficiency of

[1] Digest of evidence, *Report of the Industrial Commission*, 1900, p. 148: "Mr. Emery insists vigorously

the favored company was superior to that
of other refiners seems equally demon-
strable. By the sheer superiority of its
organization, and—so far as is known—
quite unaided by unusual discrimination
in rates, the Standard Oil Company had
obtained in 1872 its pre-eminent position.
By similar efficiency of capital and ability
other members of the South Improvement
Company had survived and grown, while
their poorer competitors had suffered from
depression. From the railway point of
view, then, the situation in 1872 justified
a special contract; and in the South Improvement Company was presented the
fittest party to such a contract.

Whether the rebate provided by the
contract excessively rewarded the company for its services as "evener" is a question of fact, not to be settled off-hand.
The violent popular uprising, the quick-

that it would have been absolutely impossible for
any one else to secure the amount of business necessary to meet this requirement of railways."

ness with which the contract was withdrawn by the railroads, the reticence and subsequent penitence of all concerned in making it, and the odium in which it has since been held by both friends and enemies of the Standard Oil Company may indeed be regarded as evidence that its provisions were unwarranted. The principle of the contract, however—the combination of both the railways and the strongest refiners to restore profitable stability to traffic and industry—was inevitable in the practice and theory of railway economics.

The panic caused in 1872 by publishing the contract of the South Improvement Company, though never more than fright —for the contract was never kept—still seemed to make the situation more acute. Under the stress of such difficult conditions, small concerns gave place to large, and large concerns combined into yet greater ones. Throughout 1872, 1873, and 1874 small refiners were driven into

34

insolvency or forced into selling. The causes assigned for this are two. "The over-production of 1873, 1874, and 1875," explains a leading opponent of the Standard Oil Company, "and the consequent almost entire destruction of petroleum values gave the Standard Oil Company, with its organization and capital, almost the desired monopoly."[1] Discrimination in freight rates in favor of the large refiners was the other and more aggravating cause. For, though they never resumed the contract of the South Improvement Company, nevertheless, at the solicitation of refiners who had signed the agreement of March 25, 1872, the railroads soon resumed the practice of increasing traffic by giving special rates to the large shippers;[2]

[1] Letter of the Delegation of Oil Producers, delivered to the Pennsylvania Railroad September 11, 1877. Quoted in *Investigation of Trusts*, Congress, 1888, p. 363.

[2] George R. Blanchard, of the Erie Railroad ("*Hepburn*" *Report*, New York, 1879, p. 3394):

"I was then convinced . . . that the agreement of

and, though their motives were — so far
as evidence is shown—thoroughly self-in-

March 25 lasted less than two weeks, and that at
an early date the Empire Line [later the great rival
of the Standard] was receiving a large drawback or
commission from the Pennsylvania Railroad, which
was either being shared with the shippers or an additional amount was being allowed to them. . . . It
is, therefore, clear that one of the largest shippers
who signed that March agreement did not feel that
it bound him to pay the rates he had agreed to
pay; and he gave convincing reasons to believe that
others, signers and parties to that agreement, did
not pay them, and possessed equal or greater advantages by way of rival routes. . . . I opened negotiations to increase our traffic, which resulted in an
agreement, with the concurrence of the Atlantic and
Great Western, as follows:

"ERIE RAILWAY CO.,
"OFFICE OF SECOND VICE-PRESIDENT,
"NEW YORK, *March* 29, 1873.

"MEMORANDUM

"Between Mr. John D. Archbold [of the Stand-
ard], Mr. Bennett, and Mr. Porter, and Mr. Osborn,
and myself. Rate for March, '73, to be 132½ from
Union [published rate, $1.65]. Rate thereafter to
be $1.25 from same point as the maximum for 1873.
If the common-point rate is made from Titusville at
any time in 1873, on *bona fide* shipments, Erie and
Atlantic and Great Western will make same rate
from same date. With this rate the refiners agree

36

terested,[1] they hastened the absorption of
the small refineries by the larger, and especially the expansion of the Standard Oil

to give us their entire product to New York for the
year, and the preference always at same rate as
actual shipment by other lines.

" (Signed)

"JOHN D. ARCHBOLD.

"G. R. BLANCHARD.

". . . I also learned at that time that this producers' agreement [of March 25] was exploded by
the action of the Producers' Union before that time.
. . . These facts effectually refute the testimony of
Mr. Patterson, that the agreement of March 25 continued more than two years, or any period beyond
three weeks, at the rates it stipulated, and show
that at least two of its signers did not feel bound to
pay the rates it named, and that they and others
by other lines endeavored immediately after it was
signed to obtain, and did secure, reduced rates, as
usual before its execution, and peddled oil among
the railroads wherever they could secure an advantage, however small, over each other on the railroads."

[1] Mr. Paul de Rousiers has suggested that the
motives of the railroad might have been mixed;
that their act might have been inspired by inevitable
railway policy reinforced by bribes from the Standard Oil Company. No proven case of bribery is
recorded, however, by any investigating committee,
commission, or court.

Company, which was the largest of all. To profit by these discriminations, and immediately by the advantages of concentrated capital, the Standard Oil Company of Ohio increased its capital stock in 1872 to $2,500,000, and in the same year combined with the Standard Oil Company of Pittsburg, the Cleveland Standard Refinery, the Pittsburg Refinery, the Atlantic Refining Company of Philadelphia, and Charles Pratt & Co. of New York—all leading independent refiners—into the Standard "alliance,"[1] which ten years later was to be the basis of the Standard Oil Trust. "It was a union, not of corporations, but of their stockholders," says the solicitor of the Standard Oil Company. "The several companies continued to conduct their business as before. They ceased to be competitive with one another in the sense of

[1] The official name of the "alliance" was the Central Association of Refiners, Mr. John D. Rockefeller, president, and Mr. Charles Pratt, secretary and treasurer.

striving to undersell one another. They continued to be competitors in the sense that each strove to show at the end of each year the best results in making the best product at low cost. From time to time new persons and additional capital were taken into this association. Whenever and wherever a man showed himself skilful and useful in any branch of the business, he was sought after. As business increased, new corporations were formed in various States, in the same interest, some as trading companies, some as manufacturing companies." [1] The motives of the combination, as stated by Mr. Dodd, were all owing to conditions prevalent in the period from 1870 till 1874. "Railroad rates were excessive and lacking in uniformity. When refiners were able to combine and throw a large volume of business to any particular road, they would get favorable rates. The rebate-and-drawback

[1] S. C. T. Dodd, *Combinations.*

system was then universal, and was not confined to oil. Undoubtedly this fact had much to do with the combination of refiners above referred to, and which came to be known as the Standard. But it was by no means the only reason. The men in control of that combination foresaw that a business which had thus far been disastrous would require co-operation on a large scale." [1]

By early developments of its refining capacity, then, the Standard Oil Company had succeeded in 1870 in controlling four per cent. of the production of the oil regions. By 1871 it had so availed itself of the competition between the trunk lines as to enjoy rates equal to those of the refiners at Pittsburg. In the depression of 1872 it had unsuccessfully essayed, with other refiners, to act as "evener" for the railroads. Frustrated in this attempt, it had returned to its policy of concentration

[1] S. C. T. Dodd, *Combinations*.

—purchasing small refineries, uniting with large ones, and exacting of the railroads discriminations proportionate to its size. By 1874 the capital of the Standard Oil Company of Ohio had been increased to $3,500,000. The control of the Standard "alliance" had been extended over more than half the refining industry, and the combination was ready to enter upon the purchase of pipe-lines. The railroads had not conspired to cause this development,[1] neither could sharp practice in competition account for it. This remarkable increase since 1870 in industrial efficiency must be due to superior ability and capital. This still more striking increase in advantages of transportation must be due to the same causes, coupled with peculiar opportunities of geographical location and railway conditions. Five years after this supremacy was accomplished, William H. Van-

[1] It has frequently been stated, though never proved, that railroad officials were financially interested in the Standard Oil Company.

derbilt, in reply to a question before the Hepburn Committee, set forth what seems on the whole the true explanation:

"*Question*. Can you attribute, or do you attribute in your own mind, the fact of there being one refiner instead of fifty now to any other cause except the larger capital of the Standard Oil Company?

"*Answer*. There are a great many causes: it is not from their capital alone that they have built up this business. There is no question about it but that these men—and if you come into contact with them I guess you will come to the same conclusion I have long ago—I think they are smarter fellows than I am, a good deal. They are very enterprising and smart men. I never came in contact with any class of men as smart and as able as they are in their business, and I think that a great deal is to be attributed to that.

"*Q*. Would that alone monopolize a business of that sort?

"*A*. It would go a great ways towards building it up. They never could have got in the position they are in now without a great deal of ability, and one man would hardly have been able to do it; it is a combination of men.

THE STANDARD OIL COMPANY

"*Q.* Wasn't it a combination that embraced the smart men in the railways as well as the smart men in the Standard Company?

"*A.* I think those gentlemen, from their shrewdness, have been able to take advantage of the competition that existed between the railroads for their business, as it grew, and that they have availed themselves of it there is no question of doubt.

"*Q.* Don't you think they have also been able to make their affiliations with railroad companies and railroad officers?

"*A.* I have not heard it charged that any railway official had any interest in any of their companies, only that I have seen in the papers, some years ago, that I had an interest in it.

"*Q.* Your interest in your railway is so large a one that nobody would conceive, as a matter of personal interest, that you would have an interest antagonistic to your road?

"*A.* When they came to do business with us in any magnitude that is the reason I disposed of my interest.

"*Q.* And that is the only way you can account for the enormous monopoly that has grown up?

"*A.* Yes; they are very shrewd men. I don't believe that by any legislative enactment or anything else, through any of the States or all

43

of the States, you can keep such men down. You can't do it! They will be on top all the time. You see if they are not." ["*Hepburn*" *Report*, New York, 1879, p. 2605.]

1874-77

By its economies in refining, attained as early as 1870 — and in freight rates, the reward of its predominance in the industry in 1872 — the Standard Oil Company in 1873 escaped in great measure the depression which harassed its competitors. This depression, if continued, promised to be disastrous both to the newly formed "alliance" and to its dwindling competitors. In the interest of both parties, therefore, relief was sought in the restriction of the oil production. Throughout 1873 there was a disposition on the part of the producers outside the region of the great wells to suspend operations. In 1874, because of the small inducement to continue, there was an important shut-

44

down in Clarion County.[1] But these methods of relief were unavailing. Throughout 1874 the weaker refineries were forced to sell to the stronger, who reduced the over-production at once by dismantling their works, so that in 1874 there were "in the oil regions proper but few refineries, and those universally owned by the Standard Oil Company, those at Pittsburg being owned or controlled by that combination, or by the Conduit and Empire lines.[2] By its supremacy in the oil regions, then, the Standard Oil Company in 1874 had added to its economies in efficiency and in transportation by rail the advantage of restricting over-production, and in the period from 1874 till 1877 was ready to add the advantage of controlling the pipe-lines.

In 1869 the first extended system of

[1] P. C. Boyle, *Report of the Industrial Commission*, 1900, p. 427.
[2] B. B. Campbell, *Investigation of Trusts*, Congress, 1888, p. 364.

pipe-lines—the Mutual Pipe-Line—was
laid in Clarion County. At the same time
William H. Abbott and Henry Harley,
with a capital of $2,000,000, were or-
ganizing into the Pennsylvania Transportation Company the five hundred miles
of pipe centring at the Miller farm. Vandergrift & Forman were establishing in
Butler County a system which was later to
be the nucleus of the United Pipe-Line
System, and the American Transfer Company and the Empire Transportation Company were forming. Such systems, however, were rare until 1874. Most of the
pipe-lines were scarcely ten miles long,
and extended from Clarion River to some
common point of shipment, where stated
freight rates were given. Their over-capacity had become so excessive, their competition so ill-considered, and their sol-
vency so much a matter of doubt that by
1874 most of them had been united into
the system of Vandergrift & Forman, the
Pennsylvania Transportation Company,

46

the Columbia Conduit Company, or the
American Transfer Company. Vandergrift & Forman at that time controlled
twenty-five or thirty per cent. of the pipe-
line traffic in the oil regions, and the five
companies together controlled by far the
greater part of the traffic.[1] Such was the
situation when the Standard Oil Company
took a hand in the business.

In 1874 the firm of Vandergrift & Forman was reorganized. Its name was
changed to the United Pipe-Line Company; and its officers were Mr. Vandergrift, president, and six officials of the
Standard "alliance" among its nine directors.[2] In the same year the five great
systems of pipe-lines agreed upon a uniform schedule of charges,[3] and the patrons
of these systems were allowed special discriminations by the railroads. This new

[1] E. C. Patterson, "*Hepburn*" *Report*, New York,
1879, p. 1693.   [2] Ibid.
[3] W. T. Scheide, "*Hepburn*" *Report*, New York,
1879, p. 2769.

47

adjustment contained in the "Rutter Circular" of September 9, 1874, raised the
charges for transportation of oil nearly
to the rates fixed by the contract of the
South Improvement Company, and al·
lowed a rebate of 22 cents on all oil coming
from the five great systems of pipe-lines
which maintained the uniform schedule of
charges.[1] By this new tariff the organiza-

---

[1] The "Rutter Circular" fixed the following rates
on refined and crude oil:
"The rates on refined oil from all refineries at
Cleveland, Titusville, and elsewhere in and adjacent
to the oil regions shall be as follows:

	Per barrel.
"To Boston	$2.10
Philadelphia	1.85
Baltimore	1.85
New York	2.00

"Net rate on Albany, fifteen per cent. less, from
which shall be refunded the amount paid for the
transportation of crude oil by rail from the mouth of
the pipes to the said refineries upon the basis of fourteen barrels of crude oil to the refineries for every
ten barrels of refined oil forwarded by rail from them
[the refineries] to the Eastern points named.
"Settlements of this drawback to be made on the
refined oil forwarded during each month.

tion of the remaining lines into one or another system was considerably hastened; and in this process of bringing order into the confused net-work of pipe-lines the Standard "alliance," the United Pipe-Line Company, owned by the Standard Oil Company, and the great systems and their patrons are greatly benefited. With the railway companies the purpose was merely to put an end to the unreliable service of the small pipe-lines, and to secure for themselves a larger and more certain traffic. With the pipe-lines, however—

"No rebate on these rates will be paid on oil reaching refineries direct by pipes.

"On crude oil the rates from all initial points of rail shipments in the oil region shall be as follows:

"To Boston, $1.75 per barrel.

"To New York, $1.50 per barrel (net rate on Albany fifteen per cent. less).

"To Philadelphia, $1.50 per barrel.

"To Baltimore, $1.50 per barrel.

"From which shall be refunded 22 cents per barrel only on oil coming from pipes which maintain the agreed rates of pipeage. A barrel shall in all cases be computed at forty-five gallons." . . .—*Investigation of Trusts*, Congress, 1888, p. 363.

49

though each of the allied pipe-lines and every refiner who was served by them shared impartially in the rebate[1]—the effect was particularly to build up the larger pipe-line and the larger refiner at the expense of the smaller. For this reason the economies in transportation by rail and pipe-line effected in 1874 tended greatly to increase the predominance of the United Pipe-Line Company and the Standard "alliance."

In the year following the United Pipe-Line Company acquired, by purchase, the greater part of the pipe-lines which had not participated in the agreement. Combinations among the large systems—the United Pipe-Line Company, the Columbia Conduit Company, and the Empire Transportation Company—gradually absorbed all the others. Meanwhile the pipe-lines enjoying the discriminations so abused their privilege by high charges that in 1875

[1] W. T. Scheide, "*Hepburn*" *Report*, New York, 1879, pp. 2770, 2794.

competition from without and suspicion within broke up the agreement. In 1874 the Baltimore and Ohio Railroad had entered Chicago and was making advances to the Columbia Conduit Company. The railway situation was uneasy; and when, in 1875, the Erie Railroad accused the Pennsylvania Railroad of granting secret discriminations to the Empire Transportation Company, the agreement among the pipe-lines was immediately broken. The Columbia Conduit Company attached itself to the Baltimore and Ohio Railroad; the Empire Transportation attached itself to the Pennsylvania Railroad;[1] and the United Pipe-Line Company, through its owner, the Standard Oil Company, completed an agreement with the Erie and the New York Central railroads, according to which it gave to each road fifty per cent. of its

---

[1] A copy of the contract between the Empire Transportation Company and the Pennsylvania Railroad is contained in the *Investigation of Trusts*, Congress, 1888, p. 210.

traffic, guaranteed to the Erie Railroad twenty-seven per cent. of the entire oil traffic in the oil regions—which was the proportion the Erie Railroad had received under the "Rutter Circular"—and received in return upon all shipments a rebate of ten per cent.[1] The motives of the Erie and the New York Central railroads were plain. Entering the oil regions by connections from the north, these roads depended entirely for their traffic upon the Standard Oil Company at Cleveland. Accordingly, for the guarantee that its oil traffic would not be diminished the Erie Railroad could afford to pay roundly; and for the maintenance of the oil industry at Cleveland, and for the privilege of handling all its traffic, the New York Central Railroad was ready to grant a liberal discrimination. Therefore, throughout the rest of 1875 all the pipe-lines in the oil regions arrayed themselves with one or another of

[1] The details of this contract are contained in the "*Hepburn*" *Report*, New York, 1879, pp. 175, 182.

the three rival pipe-lines and their allied railroads;[1] and the armed peace thus maintained continued throughout 1876.

In 1877, with the aid of the Pennsylvania Railroad, the Empire Transportation Company secured control of a refinery at Communipaw, and began constructing others at Philadelphia. The roads in alliance with the Standard Oil Company were the first to discover the encroachment, and resented it before the Standard Oil Company had time to act. "Unless checked," said Mr. Blanchard, of the Erie Railroad, "the result would be a diversion largely of the transportation of oil from our roads. The New York Central road and our own determined that we ought not to stand by and permit these improvements and arrangements to be made, which, when completed, would be beyond our control. We determined, therefore, to make the issue with the Pennsylvania Railroad Com-

[1] W. T. Scheide, "*Hepburn*" *Report*, New York, 1879, p. 2795; J. C. Welch, Ibid., p. 3673.

pany."[1] At the suggestion of the railroads, accordingly, the Standard Oil Company, by ceasing on March 18, 1877, to send freight over the Pennsylvania Railroad, precipitated a war between the great pipe-lines and their allied roads.

The suddenness and fury of the war for the oil traffic which followed is explained only by the strained relations of the trunk lines at that time. Since 1874, when the Baltimore and Ohio Railroad entered Chicago, there had been a ruinous war of rates. Freight charges during this period from Chicago to the seaboard had fallen from $1 to 10 cents. New York Central and the Erie railroads had lost millions, and the Baltimore and Ohio and the Pennsylvania railroads had ceased to pay dividends.[2] The struggle in the oil region was,

[1] G. R. Blanchard, *"Hepburn" Report*, New York, 1879, p. 1463.
[2] *Report of the "Hepburn" Committee*, New York, 1879, p. 33

54

therefore, merely part of a contest extending half across the continent. Beginning fully a month before the larger contest approached settlement, it continued bitterly for six months until the very last agreements had been signed. In this struggle the Columbia Conduit Company connected with a branch of the Reading Railroad, and controlled the traffic in the newly discovered Bradford district. The Empire Transportation Company, meanwhile, aided by the Pennsylvania Railroad, sought by a tremendous effort to crush the United Pipe - Line Company and the Standard Oil Company. The Pennsylvania Railroad carried oil at 8 cents a barrel less than cost,[1] and ordered the refineries of the Empire Transportation Company to sell oil in the territory of the Standard   alliance" at any price. But the Standard Oil Company, with its high degree of mechanical efficiency, its well-organized united pipe-

[1] Digest of the *Report of the Industrial Commission,* 1900, p. 150.

line system, and its firm alliance with the Erie and the New York Central railroads, proved superior. On October 17, 1877, the Pennsylvania Railroad was forced to abandon the struggle and to sign a contract which gave the Standard Oil Company practically the monopoly of the production and transportation of oil in the United States. According to this contract the Standard Oil Company was appointed "evener," to apportion oil traffic in the following ratio: sixty-three per cent. of the oil traffic was to go to New York City and thirty-seven per cent. to Philadelphia and Baltimore; of the traffic going to New York City, the New York Central, the Erie, and the Pennsylvania railroads were each to carry one-third; of the traffic going to Philadelphia and Baltimore, the Pennsylvania Railroad was to carry seventy per cent. and the Baltimore and Ohio thirty per cent. By the terms of the contract the Pennsylvania Railroad was guaranteed an annual traffic of not less than two million barrels;[1] and the Empire Transportation Company was purchased for $3,000,000 by the

[1] In a letter of October 17, 1877, Mr. William Rockefeller set forth this contract in five provisions, the last providing as follows for the remuneration of the Standard Oil Company:

"We ask, in consideration of the above-named guarantee of the business upon which it is understood we shall pay such rates as may be fixed from time to time by the four trunk lines (which rate, it is understood, shall be so fixed by the trunk lines as to place us on a parity as to cost of production with shippers by competing lines), that you shall furnish us promptly all the transportation we may reasonably require, and that you shall allow to and pay us weekly such commission on our own shipments and the shipments which we may control as may be agreed to by your company and the other trunk lines from time to time. This commission, it is understood, has for the present been fixed at ten per cent. upon the rate, and shall not be fixed at a less percentage, except by a mutual agreement of your company and ours; provided that no other shipper of oil by your line shall pay less than the rate fixed for us before such commission is deducted, and no commission shall be allowed any other shipper unless he shall guarantee and furnish such amount of oil for shipment as will, after deduction of commission allowed him, realize to you the same amount of profit you realize from our trade—that is, you will not allow any other shipper of oil any part of such commission, unless after such commission you realize

57

Standard Oil Company and the United
Pipe-Line Company.[1]   The Standard Oil

from the total of his business the same total of profit
you realize from the total of our business, except so
far as your company may be compelled to fill certain
contracts for transportation made by the Empire
Line with refineries and producers, which contracts
terminate on or before May 1, 1878—a statement
of which shall accompany your reply to the letter;
such contracts to be fulfilled.   We agree that all the
stipulation herein contained shall be carried out by
us for the period of five years from the date hereof."
. . .—*Investigation of Trusts*, Congress, 1888, p. 208.

[1] The motives of this act have been thus stated:
"It was the desire on the part of the Pennsylvania
Railroad to have a portion of our other business
that induced them to bring about this negotiation
with the Empire Transportation Company, and we
yielded to their most urgent persuasions.   We did
not want the property, but they insisted upon it
that we should buy it.   We did finally yield to their
persuasions, and purchased that portion of the Empire Transportation Company's property, meaning
the local pipe-lines in the oil regions.   We had stated
in early discussions with representatives of the Pennsylvania Railroad that we were willing to buy the
refineries owned by the Empire Transportation
Company; but, as we were not interested in transportation at all, we wanted them to pay for the pipe-
lines and own them themselves.   But we yielded
that point finally."—H. M. Flagler, of the Standard
Oil Company, *Investigation of Trusts*, 1888, p. 773.

Company, meanwhile, for its services as "evener" was remunerated in the following fashion: After May 1, 1878, when the contracts between the Pennsylvania Railroad and its shippers expired, the Standard Oil Company received a rebate of ten per cent. on all its freight. In addition to this it was allowed, with other shippers, a rebate of 68½ cents in order that it might be on an equality with those refineries who shipped by the Erie Canal; and the American Transfer Company, which had now been united with the United Pipe-Line Company, was allowed 22½ cents as its share of the through rate.

The Pennsylvania Railroad offered to carry oil for *all* shippers on these terms, except that for the ten per cent. rebate it asked such considerations as the Standard alone could furnish; and, indeed, for those refiners who made all their shipments over its line, it continued to give rates as low as those of the Standard Oil Company. On December 8, 1878, however, when the Erie

59

Canal was closed, the railroad ceased making such favorable rates for independent refiners; and on March 31, 1879, all payments of rebates ceased.[1]

In view of the bitterness of the war

[1] A. J. Cassatt, testimony in Commonwealth of Pennsylvania *v.* Pennsylvania Railroad. Quoted in "*Hepburn*" *Report*, New York, 1879, pp. 483–519. Summarized by Archbold, *Report of the Industrial Commission*, 1900, p. 1515.

Expressed statistically, the rates and rebates of May 1, 1878, are:

Tariff rate on crude oil		. $1.40
Allowance to American Transfer Company	$0.225	
Allowance to Standard Oil Company, ten per cent. . . .	0.14	
Allowance to Standard Oil Company	0.15	0.515
Net rate to Standard Oil Company		. $0.885
Tariff rate on refined oil		. 1.90
Rebate to all shippers	$0.645	
Rebate to Standard Oil Company.	0.455	1.10
Net rate to Standard Oil Company.		. $0.80
Net rate to other shippers		. 1.255

Mr. Cassatt testified that large independent re-

which it settled, this agreement was very
favorable to the defeated party. The
Pennsylvania Railroad had gone out of its
way to strike at the power of the Standard
"alliance," and after expensive fighting
had been completely beaten and forced to
sue for such terms as might mercifully be
granted it. The Standard Oil Company,
however, required of it only such favors
as it already received of the New York
Central and the Erie railroads, and, in return, guaranteed its oil traffic, purchased
its interest in the Empire Transportation
Company, and advanced the money to
buy oil-cars. It was, indeed, shrewd mag-
nanimity; for, in advancing the money to
complete the sale, the Standard Oil Company became the mortgager of the oil-cars
of the railroad,[1] and by aid of the discriminations provided in the contract it was

finers usually receive secret rebates, which sometimes equal those of the Standard Company.
    [1] H. M. Flagler, *Investigation of Trusts*, Congress,
1888, pp. 770–774.

able, in a few months, to drive the Columbia Conduit Company into selling.[1] So that in 1878 and 1879 the Standard Oil Company owned or controlled by contract every transporting agent in the oil regions.

The achievement of this supremacy marks the close of the first phase of the Standard Oil Company. It owned the terminal facilities of the New York Central for handling oil at New York. It leased the terminal facilities of the Erie Railroad at New York. It owned or leased almost all the oil-cars on the Erie, the New York Central, and the Pennsylvania railroads.[2] Through the United Pipe-Line Company and the American Transfer Company, it purchased, one after another, twenty-six pipe-lines that threatened competition.[3]

[1] John C. Welch, "*Hepburn*" *Report*, New York, 1879, p. 3671.
[2] *Report of the* "*Hepburn*" *Committee*, New York, 1879, p. 40.
[3] *Report of the Industrial Commission*, 1900, p. 101.

62

And when, in 1879, the Tidewater Pipe-Line Company was built to the seaboard, in order to evade the discriminations of the railways, the Standard Oil Company was able, after a struggle of four years, to defeat that also. The dominance of the Standard Oil Company in the refining industry was even more striking. In 1879 it controlled ninety-five per cent. of the refineries in the oil region, and at one time during this period there were scarcely a dozen independent refiners in business.[1]

An explicated narrative—such as this has pretended to be—should bear its own judgment upon the agents who accomplished the oil monopoly. That judgment —if the narrative has succeeded in logical clearness—runs somewhat as follows: Given the railway and economic conditions, the progress of the Standard Oil Company was quite inevitable. Since it

[1] *Report of the Industrial Commission*, 1900, p. 95.

showed at an early time bright promise of industrial efficiency, it readily acquired, after the fashion of the period, proportionate discrimination in freight rates. By getting control through discriminations of the means of transportation, it inevitably achieved monopoly. In support of this judgment it may be urged—as Mr. Paul de Rousiers boldly urges — that discriminations, "though important in the beginning, went into the background with the absorption of the pipe-lines, and, though very helpful in the creation of the trust, were not indispensable to its continuance." Conditions alone, he continues, were such as to make monopoly in some sort inevitable. "Historically it is a fact; and one does not see how otherwise it could have obtained, in so quick and complete a fashion, the result towards which it tended." If the Standard Oil Company were not the strongest refiner, its most powerful rival would certainly have seized the same control over transportation that the Standard

Oil Company in fact secured. In the last analysis, monopoly by the Standard Oil Company was, under existing conditions, inevitable, simply because it was most efficiently organized.

II

1877–83

THE organization of the Standard "alliance," which in 1879 controlled the transportation of oil by rail and by pipe-line and produced ninety-five per cent. of the refined oil of the country, was an informal substitute for the modern trust. The bond of unity was common ownership of stock in the various companies of the "alliance" and personal agreement between the officers of the respective companies and the officers of the Standard Oil Company.[1] The Standard "alliance" included the Standard Oil Company of Cleveland, the Standard Company of Pittsburg, the Acme Oil Company of New York (located

---

[1] *"Hepburn" Report*, 1879, p. 2614.

at Titusville), the Imperial Oil Company
at Oil City, the Atlantic Refining Company
of Philadelphia, the Camden Company of
Maryland, Charles Pratt & Co. of New
York, J. A. Bostwick & Co., Sone & Flem-
ing Manufacturing Company, Warden,
Frew & Co. of Philadelphia, and the Baltimore United Oil Company of Baltimore.[1]
The petroleum producers, on the other hand,
had meantime been organizing to stay the
further progress of the Standard "alliance"
in a league which suggested in its forms a
revival of the fifteenth-century guild.

In 1877 local lodges of the fraternal General Council of the Petroleum Producers'
Union had been formed, under the strictest
obligations of secrecy, throughout the oil
region. Eventually, from two thousand
five hundred to three thousand producers
were enrolled as members in the local
lodges, which sent delegates to the General Council. The object of the union was

[1] *"Hepburn" Report,* 1879. pp. 42, 2615.

"the collection and dissemination of valuable information respecting the production, storing or tanking, shipping, refining, and consumption of petroleum; the securing the most advantageous facilities for transportation; the protection of the producing interests against unfriendly legislation and unjust exactions; the correction of all abuses and pernicious practices detrimental to the producing business and the improvement of the trade generally." At the first meeting of the General Council, in the Universalist church in Titusville, November 21, 1877, Mr. Benjamin B. Campbell, a well-known opponent of the Standard, was elected president; and standing committees were chosen on finance, reports and statistics, transportation, pipelines, patents, refining, legislation, national legislation, and legal remedies. Once a month the General Council met regularly at Titusville.[1]

[1] *Investigation of Trusts*, House Reports, First

The first aim of the society was to stop
the drilling of new wells and to induce producers to provide storage for their oil, in
order that they might not be subject to
the necessity of forced sales. Throughout
northwestern Pennsylvania, in the counties of Alleghany, Armstrong, Butler, Clarion, Venango, Crawford, and Warren, this
object was effected; and, "had it not been
for the unusual development of the oil-
field in McKean County," as the report
of the General Council naïvely explains,
these efforts might have succeeded. But
"the producers continued to crowd each
other with new wells and to rely solely
upon the United Pipe-Line to furnish storage and local transportation. The result was that the eager driller of wells
found his product at the mercy of the pur-
chaser, and was speedily subjected to low
prices and loss of oil." [1] Of more impor-

Session, Fiftieth Congress, 1887–88, ix., p. 692; a
copy of the constitution is given, p. 47.

[1] *Investigation of Trusts*, Congress, 1888, p. 692.

tance were the efforts of the society to secure transportation facilities. At a time
when the transportation agents, both local and to the seaboard, were in alliance
with the Standard interests, the Equitable
Petroleum Company, formed by the producers of McKean County to provide an
outlet by pipe-line to the McKean and
Buffalo Railroad, thence to Buffalo, and
by way of the Erie Canal to New York,
was enthusiastically encouraged by the
General Council. The committee on legislation meanwhile had introduced into
Congress and into the Pennsylvania Legislature bills regulating the companies
engaged in the transportation of petroleum. These proposals, however, were
not well received; and in its report in
1878 the disgruntled committee, describ-
ing its labors, said: "It has been simply a history of failure and disgrace.
If it has taught us anything, it is
that our present law-makers are, as a
body, ignorant, corrupt, and unprinci-

pled." [1] So far, in spite of all its activity,
the General Council had brought no practical relief to the producers; so that when,
in May, 1878, the committee on legal
remedies advised resort to whatever existing laws there might be, the council at
once authorized the committee to take the
necessary steps.

The committee immediately laid its
grievances before the attorney - general;
and on behalf of the committee the at-
torney-general brought action against the
United Pipe-Line Company for the forfeiture of its charter, and prayed for an injunction restraining the Pennsylvania
Railroad, the Atlantic and Great Western
Railroad, the Lake Shore and Michigan
Southern Railroad, and the Dunkirk, Alleghany and Pittsburg Railroad from "com-
bining to create and perpetuate a monopoly of the oil business, from granting un-
reasonable rebates to the Standard Oil

---

[1] *Investigation of Trusts*, Congress, 1888, p. 693.

71

Company and its allies, from refusing cars to shippers, from breaking connections with other roads, from buying and selling petroleum in connection with the Standard combination, from refusing transportation, from making discriminations in form of one shipper against another, and from granting greater facilities to one than to another."

Amid great popular excitement at Bradford these proceedings were decided upon. Mass-meetings were held, processions paraded the streets, and riot seemed imminent. The recent months had been marked by heavy depression in the oil trade and bitter antagonism of producers and oil buyers. Riotous meetings were held before the United Pipe-Line Company's offices; men were hanged in effigy; and processions of masked men marched the streets, and groaned and hooted before the offices of the buyers. Numerous secret societies were formed among the producers; and every morning the streets and

sidewalks were found placarded with cab-
alistic signs and proclamations. About
this time occurred the investigation of railroads in New York by the Hepburn Committee of the legislature; and a similar
investigation of the petroleum trade in
Pennsylvania was being urged. In the
popular frenzy of the moment all the officers of the Standard Oil Company were in-
dicted for conspiracy in restraint of trade,
and requisition made to the Governor to
secure their extradition from New York.[1]

All these troubles arose from the depression incident to the excessive production of the McKean County wells, which
was greater than the capacity of the storage-tanks. The storage-tanks were built
by the pipe-line companies under contract
with the producers to "carry in its system
of pipes and tanks an amount of petroleum
not exceeding the capacity of the tanks."

The Pipe-Line Company, after due no-

[1] *Investigation of Trusts*, Congress, 1888, p. 706.

73

tice that the surplus production exceeded
its ability to construct tanks for storage,
finally announced that while it would continue to take oil for immediate shipment
it could take no more for storage except as
storage capacity was created by shipments.
The producers, in order to save oil from
running to waste at their wells, were forced
to sell it at reduced price to refiners who
would immediately ship the same or an
equivalent amount from the pipe-line
tanks. This enabled the Standard to purchase "immediate shipment" at a lower
rate than "certificate" oil, because the
latter had the privilege of remaining in
storage. Immediate shipment seems to
have been an absolute necessity so far as
the Pipe-Line was concerned, and the
lower price was the inevitable result of
over-production, which soon affected "certificate" as well as "immediate shipment"
oil. For a time the claim of over-production and want of storage capacity was denied by the producers, but this eventually

became too apparent for dispute. By extraordinary effort, however, and the ex-
penditure of millions of capital, the Pipe-
Line Company finally erected sufficient
tankage to hold the accumulated surplus
of oil; and the producers in due time were
satisfied.

In the suit which was brought against
the United Pipe-Line Company, asking for
the forfeiture of its charter on the ground
that it had made discriminations in pipeage, it appeared that, so far as any discriminations existed, they were due to contracts
for special rates inherited from the lines
which had recently been absorbed in the
company—among them, curiously enough,
one between a member of the prosecuting
committee of the Producers' Union and
the Mutual Pipe-Line Company.[1] These
discriminations were recognized by the
Standard to be contrary to public policy, and were at once discontinued. The

[1] *Report of the Industrial Commission*, 1900, i., pp.
476–479.

grievance for which the producers had brought prosecution against the railroads was a shipping agreement between the Standard and the railroads. This agreement provided that, since the Standard shipped ninety per cent. or more of the crude petroleum of the region, it might make requisition at any time for that per cent. of the oil-cars of the railroad. The producers maintained, however, that, since the Standard owned already a large number of private cars running on the railroads, it ought not to be allowed its *pro rata* allotment of the railroad's cars upon demand; particularly when, as happened at this time, the ten per cent. of railroad oil-cars was insufficient to transport the oil which independent producers wished to ship. The demands of the producers were unusual, and the refusal of the transportation companies to grant them seems quite within their rights. When it is considered that, meantime, propositions were being made to the producers by the Standard, according to which the price of crude oil should be based upon the relative price of refined, it would seem that a fair attempt, at least, had been made to satisfy the producing interest.[1] Indeed, the issue of those suits proved them to be merely the ebullition of excited popular feeling. The indictment of conspiracy against the officers of the Standard was continued, and eventually dropped.[2] The suits against the Pennsylvania Railroad and against the United Pipe-Line Company were protracted,[3] and finally dismissed by an agreement among all parties; and with the passing of this period of litigation the importance of the Petroleum Producers' Union practically ended.

In 1881 the Standard Oil Company of Ohio, the nucleus of the Standard "alliance," was a corporation capitalized at $3,500,000. Since the formation of the "alliance" it had maintained connections

---

[1] *Investigation of Trusts*, Congress, 1888, p. 694.
[2] Ibid., p. 710.   [3] Ibid., p. 711.

77

with its allies by a union, not of corporations, but of stockholders. "Then," as the solicitor of the Standard Oil Company explains, "for convenience of control and management the Standard Oil Trust was formed. It was simply an agreement, placing all the stock of these various companies in the hands of trustees, declaring the terms on which they were held, and providing for the issuance of a certificate showing the amount of each owner's interest in the stock so held in trust. This agreement did not in any essential manner change the character of the association previously existing. Its essential character was simply a common ownership of stock in various corporations. If they had so preferred, the owners of these several associated companies could have organized—in the State of New York, for example—with any capitalization desired. Each could then have lawfully combined with all the other companies, forming one corporation to transact business wherever

78

desired. But it seemed preferable, instead of organizing one corporation in New York, to organize a corporation in each State where business was being carried on, so that the business transacted in each State might be conducted by a home corporation, subject in all respects to the law of the State where located. Accordingly, we organized a Standard Oil Company in New York, in New Jersey, in Kentucky, in Iowa, in Minnesota; and similar corporations already existed in Ohio and Pennsylvania." [1]

As the first "trust" form of combination, the agreement under which this union was brought about deserves attention. There were three classes of parties to the contract: first, all the stockholders and members of the Standard "alliance," together with members of some other companies; second, all the more important officers and stockholders of these several

[1] S. C. T. Dodd, quoted in *Trusts or Competition*, edited by A. B. Nettleton, Chicago, 1900, p. 197.

companies; and, third, a portion of the stockholders and members of some additional corporations and limited partnerships. Provision was made for the admission of new companies and individuals, and for the formation, whenever advisable, of a Standard Oil Company in any State or Territory in the Union. The parties of the several classes were to transfer all their property to the Standard Oil Companies in their several States, in consideration of which they should receive stock equal at par value to the appraised value of the property so transferred.[1] This stock — and here is the significant feature of the new organization—was to be delivered to trustees, and held by them and their suc-

[1] The thirty-nine companies who signed the agreement were subsequently merged into twenty. The list of the original thirty-nine is given in *Investigation of Trusts*, 1888, Congress, p. 350. The list of the resulting twenty, with the appraisal of their property, is given in *Report of the Industrial Commission*, 1900, i., p. 301. The capitalization of these companies is $102,233,700: the excess of the appraisal over the capitalization is $19,397,612.63.

cessors thereafter; and no subsequent issue of stock should be made by the companies except to these trustees. In return for the stock intrusted to them, the trustees were to deliver trust certificates, equal to the par value of the stock of the several Standard Oil Companies to be established and to the appraised value of the stocks of other companies delivered to the trustees. The trustees provided for were nine in number. They were John D. Rockefeller, O. N. Payne, and William Rockefeller, elected to hold office till 1885; J. A. Bostwick, H. M. Flagler, and W. G. Warden, to hold office till 1884; and Charles Pratt, Benjamin Brewster, and John D. Archbold, to hold office till 1883. At each annual meeting the certificate owners elected three trustees, for three years each, to fill vacancies due to expiration of term. Such was the "trust" as formed by the agreement of January 2, 1882.[1]

[1] The trust agreement is given in full in *Investigation of Trusts*, Congress, 1888, p. 307.

By an amendment two days later this agreement was slightly changed, as it was deemed inexpedient that all the companies mentioned should transfer their property immediately to the several Standard Oil Companies. The trustees were given power to decide what companies should convey their property and when the sale should take place. The powers of the trustees, then, as defined by the "trust" agreement, were to collect on the stock which they held the dividends of the several constituent companies, and afterwards, upon the trust certificates outstanding, to disburse their receipts as dividends.

Four years before the formation of the trust, two pipe-line companies—the Seaboard Pipe-Line Company and the Equitable Petroleum Company—projected to afford an outlet to the seaboard, had been organized by oil producers.[1] Upon their

---

[1] *Investigation of Trusts*, Congress, 1888, p. 696.

failure, the producers organized the Tidewater Pipe-Line Company, which ran from
the Bradford region to Williamsport, a distance of one hundred and ten miles; and
thence, by a connection with the Philadelphia and Reading Railroad, the oil was
carried a distance of two hundred and
fifty miles to Philadelphia.[1] On the 1st of
June, 1879, this company commenced the
shipment of oil. The railroads were not
content to see the oil traffic slip through
their hands; and on the 5th of June, at a
conference between the four trust lines
at Niagara Falls, resolute measures were
adopted to drive this rival transportation
agent from the business. The rate on
crude oil per barrel was lowered to 20 cents
on all oil of the Standard "alliance" moving from the oil regions to New York, Philadelphia, and Baltimore.[2] A correspond-

[1] "*Hepburn*" *Report*, 1879, p. 3493; *Report of the
Industrial Commission*, 1900, i., p. 696.
[2] The rates are given in full in "*Hepburn*" *Report*,
Exhibits, 1879, pp. 621, 622.

ing reduction of the rate to the general public was made from $1.15 to 30 cents. These rates took effect at once;[1] and, as competition continued, a further reduction was made on August 1st to 15 cents per barrel.[2]

Throughout the period of the organization of the trust, and for a full year after, this fierce contest between the railroads and the Tidewater Pipe-Line Company continued. The immediate effect, of course, was to benefit the shippers, and particularly the largest shipper, which was the Standard. The ownership by the Standard of the terminal facilities and of the greater number of the oil-cars of the railroads now became a fact of importance. In consideration of its heavy investments in these interests, and of its agreement to ship and to unload its oil at its own risk, the Standard had already been allowed rebates.[3] But now the Standard began the

[1] "*Hepburn*" *Report*, 1879, p. 3688.
[2] Ibid., p. 45.   [3] Ibid., p. 1471.

building of pipe-lines to the seaboard and the formation of the National Transit Company. As pipe-lines were a cheaper mode of transportation than railways, the building of these lines made necessary a readjustment of freight rates; and, as the pipe-lines then building could not carry the oil the entire distance, contracts for joint carrying had to be made with the railroads. The first contract—made between the National Transit Company and the Pennsylvania Railroad on May 6, 1881 —related to the apportionment of the freight when the haul was partly by pipe-line and partly by rail. The Pipe-Line Company guaranteed the railroad one-third of the transportation of oil to the seaboard.[1] The Standard was to pay exactly the same rate as other shippers over the railroad. On such oil as was carried partly by pipe-line and partly by rail a through rate was made, of which the pipe-line naturally re-

[1] *Report of the Industrial Commission*, 1900, i., pp. 760–763.

85

ceived a share; and, finally, the Pipe-Line Company agreed to remit part of the charge of its local pipes to the railroad. Instead of a contract for rebates to the Standard, this was a contract for rebates to the railroad. The reason for this contract was that the seaboard pipe-line of the Standard did not extend beyond Hamilton, Pennsylvania; and to compensate the railroad for its low rate of freight and for its grants of rights of way—no free-pipe-line law then existing in New Jersey —these rebates were provided.

Strengthened by these mutually helpful contracts, the National Transit Company and railroads were meanwhile wearing out the Tidewater Pipe - Line Company, and in 1883 forced it to cease its opposition. The company was never absorbed by the Standard Oil Trust; but on October 9th, by an agreement with the National Transit Company, it agreed to accept as its share of the oil traffic eleven and one-half per cent. of the total pipe-line transportation

86

of petroleum to the seaboard, and was guaranteed $500,000 in annual profits for fifteen years.[1] With this settlement the war of the transportation agents ceased, and the Standard Oil Trust established itself in the strategic position which substantially controlled the transportation of oil to the seaboard. By the early seventies the Standard had attained the pre-eminence in mechanical efficiency which it has ever since maintained; by the agreement with the Pennsylvania Railroad in 1878 it had gained a dominance over transportation which it never since has lost; and by its contract in 1881 it made possible the completion of its pipe-line to the seaboard and its independence of railroads. Such contracts as the Standard subsequently made with the Pennsylvania Railroad were agreements by which the railroad got some part of the freight, though it did no part of the carrying.

[1] *Report of the Industrial Commission*, 1900, i., p. 738.

The Standard Oil Trust now gave rebates instead of receiving them. Over every branch of the industry, in 1883, it was supreme.

1883–92

From the very beginning of the oil industry in Pennsylvania, movements for the restriction of oil production had been frequent. Restriction had been the aim of the Petroleum Producers' Association at its organization in 1869. The association had maintained an agency to store all oil above a certain amount and keep it from the market. This early "shut-down" failed because of the enormous production in Butler County. Succeeding "shutdowns" in 1872, 1874, 1876, and 1878 met with similar fate. In 1884 there was another general movement among producers to restrict drilling; but, through the refusal of the operators who were running large wells in the new Thorn Creek district, the movement was only partially successful. It led, however, to the organization of the Producers' Associated Oil Company, with a capital stock enabling it, when necessary, to purchase oil property in order to curtail production.[1]

On the 1st of October, 1887, this new organization, embracing eighty-five per cent. of the fourteen thousand producers in the oil regions, agreed with the Standard Oil Company to restrict production. From June to October the Producers' Protective Association, by various secret and public meetings, had encouraged the movement. The conditions of the industry favored the organization. The accumulated stock of oil was thirty-one million barrels, prices were below the remunerative point, and the Standard was losing by the deterioration of oil in its store. After conference between the Standard and the associated producers, it was agreed that the producers

[1] *Report of the Industrial Commission*, 1900, i., pp. 426–430.

should restrict their production one-third during the following year, in consideration for which the Standard turned over to the producers six million barrels of oil, at the market price at the time of the contract, and secured to the producers the profit from the anticipated rise in prices.[1]

By this bargain the producers immediately profited. On the oil they received from the Standard they made 9 cents a gallon. Encouraged by their success, they made agreements during the next year with the Well‑drillers' Union to equalize the amount of oil produced by each individual.[2] Although it was not possible to bring all the producers into the agreement, the price of crude oil was advanced by this restriction 29 cents per barrel. The price of refined oil to consumers was advanced about three-fourths of a cent—

[1] *Investigation of Trusts*, Congress, 1888, p. 52.
[2] An account of the negotiations and copies of the contracts are given in *Investigation of Trusts*, Congress, 1888, pp. 52–60, 69. See also *Report of the Industrial Commission*, i., pp. 429–432, 459–462.

an increase somewhat less than the advance in crude oil. Although the Standard Oil Company had entered into the agreement only at the urgent request of the producers, as the chief refiner it bore the burden of the advance; and when the "shut-down" was found to be injuring the laborers employed in the drilling of wells, and the Producers' Association set aside one million barrels of oil for their relief, the Standard added another million for the same purpose. This philanthropy, in the end, proved not unprofitable. The Standard benefited by the harmony it had established; and the producers, by relieving the well-drillers, prevented them from working for producers outside the agreement.

As was to be expected, the results of this movement were only temporary. In time the "shut-down" was abandoned, but not until it had gained a great though transient benefit, and had given the impulse to the building of several pipe-lines.

To the producers the Standard had come as a pacificator, restoring harmony where before had been mutual suspicion and distress. To the refiners, however, the Standard had never appeared other than a competitor, enabled by its greater size to secure favors denied its smaller rivals. Freight discriminations, before the passage of the Industrial Commission Act in 1887, were common; all oil shippers received some rebate from the published rate, the amount varying roughly according to the favorable position of the refiner for making his bargains.[1] How completely proper this seemed to the railroad manager of that day, and how sound appeared the reasons on which it was based, is well illustrated by the decision of the Ohio court, in 1884, in a suit brought by a firm of independent refiners against the Lake Shore and Michigan Southern Railroad to prevent the granting of rebates to the Standard Oil Com-

[1] *Report of the Industrial Commission.* 1900, i., p. 790.

pany.[1] The rebates complained of, the court found, amounted to 10 cents per barrel on all the oil the Standard shipped; but the consideration for these rebates the court found in the following fact:

" Prior to 1875 it was a question whether the Standard Oil Company would remain in Cleveland or remove its works to the oil-producing country, and this question depended mainly upon rates of transportation from Cleveland to the market; prior thereto, the Standard Company shipped large quantities of its products by water to Chicago and other lake points, and from thence distributed the same by rail to inland markets; it then represented to the defendant the probability of such removal; water transportation was very low during the season of navigation; unless some arrangement was made for rates at which it could ship the year around as an inducement, it would ship by water and store for winter distribution; it owned its tank-cars and had tank stations and switches, or would have, at Chicago, Toledo, Detroit, and

<hr />

[1] *Investigation of Trusts*, Congress, 1888, p. 552. Schofield, Shurmer & Teagle *v.* Lake Shore and Michigan Southern Railroad.

Grand Rapids, on and into which the cars and oil in bulk could be delivered and unloaded without expense and annoyance to defendant; it had switches at Cleveland leading to its works at which to load cars, and would load and unload all cars; the quantity of the oil to be shipped by the company was very large, and amounted to ninety per cent. or more of all the oil manufactured or shipped from Cleveland, and, if satisfactory rates could be agreed upon, it would ship over defendant's road all its oil products for territory and markets west and northwest of Cleveland, and agree that the quantity for each year should be equal to the amount shipped the preceding year; upon the faith of these representations the defendant entered into a contract; the rates were not fixed rates, but depended upon the general card tariff rates as charged from time to time [by which its shipments were] substantially to be carried from time to time at about 10 cents per barrel less than tariff rates; in consideration of such reduced rates as to bulk oil, the Standard Company agreed to furnish its own cars and tanks, load them on switches, and unload oil shipped in barrels without expense to defendant, and, by reason thereof, with less risk to defendant; and was also to ship all its freight to points west and northwest of Cleveland (except small quantities) to lake ports not reached by rail, and so to manage the shipments as to cars and times as would be most favorable to defendant. . . .

"At a cost exceeding $100,000 the Standard Company had constructed the terminal facilities promised and herein found; in actual fact, the risk of danger from fire to defendant, the expense of handling in loading and unloading, and in the use of the standard tank-cars is less than upon oil shipped without the use of such or similar facilities; the Standard Company commenced by shipping about four hundred and fifty thousand barrels per year over defendant's road, which increased from year to year, until, in 1882, . . . the quantity so shipped on defendant's road amounted to seven hundred and forty-two thousand barrels, equal to two thousand barrels, or one full tank-load, per day.

"Said arrangements are not exclusive, but are at all times open to others shipping a like quantity and furnishing like device and facilities."

By successive contracts, the court found, this agreement was continued in 1880, 1882, and 1883; and, in conclusion, the court declared that the evidence presented supported the contention of the Standard that the advantages secured to the Standard by its contract with the railroad were not, in the accepted sense of the term, rebates, but were an equivalent for the lowered cost of freight. In so holding, the court was but following the current judgment of the time.

But there were at that time other departures from the regular tariff rates which cannot so readily be explained. Throughout 1888 there were sudden and distressing increases in the tariff rates for oil, which seriously inconvenienced the inland refiners.[1] A notorious example of such charges was found in the management of the Cleveland and Marietta Railroad by its receiver in 1885. The Standard, it appears, controlled most of the pipe-lines in the Macksburg field connecting with the several stations of the railway; and its local manager was desirous of deter-

[1] *Report of the Industrial Commission,* 1900, i., p. 157.

mining a through rate on oil from the well to Marietta. Accordingly, he arranged with the receiver of the railroad that the rate be 35 cents per barrel, and that the railroad should collect this rate and pay over to the Standard 25 cents for pipeage. This agreement was put in writing, and forwarded for approval and execution to the Standard Oil Company. Meanwhile the receiver raised the tariff rate for oil from 17½ cents to 35 cents for all shipments made over this line, with the result that one refiner, carrying his crude oil from the well to the station by his own pipe-line, was forced to pay 35 cents freight, of which 25 cents was at once to be turned over to his competitor, the Standard Oil Company, for pipeage which it had never rendered. Whether the cost of pipeage warranted so large a proportion of the through rate going to the Standard is a question which cannot be answered offhand. The indefensible method of collecting the combined pipeage and freight charges was more plain. The Standard Oil Company never carried this contract through, but sent it back to its manager with instructions to end the arrangement and refund to the shippers the amount of these wrongful rebates. This was done before suit was brought to remove the receiver.[1]

A more typical example of the rebates of this period is the contract between the National Transit Company and the Pennsylvania Railroad. According to this agreement the Transit Company, which was the transporting agent of the Standard Trust, agreed that, if out of the total amount of oil shipped to the seaboard the Pennsylvania Railroad should not have moved twenty-six per cent., the Transit Company should ship by the Pennsylvania Railroad the amount required, and the railroad should be entitled to one-half the

[1] *Report of the Industrial Commission*, 1900, i., pp. 556–559.

current rate thereon. By another contract of the same date it was provided
that, if the railroad company preferred,
the Transit Company itself would carry
this extra quantity, and would then pay to
the railway freight on the oil thus carried
by itself, after deducting 6 or 10 cents a
barrel as compensation for pipeage. In
return for these stipulations it was agreed
that all joint rates from any delivery point
of the local pipe-lines to any refining or
terminal point should be fixed by the railroad in concurrence with the Transit Company; and at the time of the agreement
this rate was fixed at 45 cents to the
seaboard.[1]

The advantage to the railroad, under
this agreement, is manifest. Throughout
the continuance of this contract, which
was the last one made and continued till
1887, there was a regular deficiency in the
share of the oil to be carried by the rail-

[1] *Report of the Industrial Commission,* 1900, i. pp.
663–666.

road, amounting in some months to eighty thousand barrels, and settled by payments of the Transit Company to the railroad.[1] Essentially it was a contract of rebate to the railways rather than of rebate to the Standard, the motives of which were similar to the contract of 1881. It was a payment to the railroad in compensation for grants of rights of way. Other pipe-lines could not get through to the seaboard because they could not make terms with the railroads. The advantage accruing to the Standard from such a contract as this was good-will, of which it stood at that time in great need. "The pipe-line was then completed to the seaboard," explains Mr. Dodd, solicitor of the Standard. "It could not have reached that point without the consent of the railway company, as no free-pipe-line law then existed in the State of Pennsylvania. It was still necessary to have a traffic contract with the railroad

[1] *Report of the Industrial Commission*, 1900, i., p. 761.

to deliver oil to the railroads at different points on the through line." Clearly the injustice of this contract, if any there be, should be laid at the door of the railways. To them rather than to the Standard did the greater benefit accrue. And if this contract, by providing that joint rates for the transportation of oil should be fixed by the railroad in concurrence with the Transit Company, opened the way to such abuses as the sudden and arbitrary raising of rates at less-important shipping points not used by the Standard, the blame belongs rather with the railroad than with the Standard Oil Company.

The passing of the Interstate Commerce Act, in 1887, makes a natural division in the record of the railroad arrangements made by the Standard. By the terms of that act discriminations were forbidden, and such contracts with shippers as had been the rule since the late sixties were made illegal. The Interstate Commerce Act seems to have been observed by the

Standard Oil Company. "Little testimony," says the Industrial Commission
of 1900, "was brought forward to prove
that it still actually receives lower rates
for shipment over the same tracks than
its competitors."[1] In the testimony before the commission on this latter point
the opinion was expressed by witnesses
testifying in opposition to the Standard
Oil Company that direct discriminations
and rebates are still received by the Standard; but the evidence adduced in proof
of this opinion was unsatisfactory, and
was considered entirely inconclusive by
the commission.[2]

[1] *Report of the Industrial Commission*, 1900, i., p.
158.

[2] Ibid., p. 159.

Apart from hearsay the only evidence produced to
prove the existence of discrimination in favor of the
Standard were the letter of the receivers of the Balti-
more and Ohio Railroad to the Interstate Commerce
Commission, December 22, 1898, and the case of
Logan, Emery, and Weaver *v.* the Pennsylvania
Railroad Company.

The letter of receivers Cowen and Murray states:
"Within the territory north of the Ohio River

In other ways than by discriminations in actual rates the Standard Oil Company, after 1887, secured special advantages in transportation. The shipments of oil from

and east of the Mississippi the railroad carriers are transporting the larger part of the interstate traffic at rates less than those shown in the published tariff filed with your commission, which are by statute the only lawful rates.

"While this condition continues there will exist the unjust discriminations between persons, localities, and particular descriptions of traffic the prevention of which is the main object of the act of establishing your commission. Only by securing the uniform charging of the published rates can the just quality of service and of charge required by law be secured either between persons or between localities." (p. 637.)

This letter doubtless sets forth a deplorable fact, but how it relates to the case of the Standard is not clear.

The Logan, Emery, and Weaver case was brought in 1887 and continued until 1890. The president and the general freight agent of the Pennsylvania Railroad both testified in 1890 that positively no rebates had been paid since 1887. But the auditors and assistant auditors of the road testified that rebates from 8 to 28 cents per barrel had been granted since 1887. From the facts of the case it appears that the Standard Oil Company was in no way concerned. Indeed, in the evidence,

those localities which it chose for distributing points were so large that the freight
rates for that locality were naturally most
favorable to this chief commodity of ship-

as cited by witnesses testifying in opposition to the
Standard, the chief recipient of the rebates was the
Bear Creek Oil Refining Company, with which B. B.
Campbell, originator of the Petroleum Producers'
Union, was associated. Mr. Campbell testified that
from October 1, 1884, until July 1, 1888, his company had received rebates on shipments from Cole-
man Station to Philadelphia, Communipaw, and
Bolivar amounting in all to $48,101. The case was
settled out of court, as the plaintiffs were too poor
to carry the suit further. A settlement was accepted according to which the railway paid $35,000 and
the costs of the suit. (pp. 633, 635, 660.)

This reported case, the only documentary evidence directly relating to discriminations in the oil
traffic, explicitly excludes the Standard Oil Company and incriminates only a leading independent
refiner.

Replying to these charges, Mr. Archbold, vice-
president of the Standard Oil Company, submitted
letters from officers of leading railways of the country in reply to a circular inquiry sent out by the
Standard Oil Company asking whether the respective roads had granted any advantages to that company "either by direct tariff, rebate, under-billing,
or in any other way." These letters specifically
deny that any such preferences have been given to

ment. Competitive points, points where several railroads compete, or where water transportation competes with the railways, were generally fixed upon as distributing centres. Accordingly, lower freight rates prevailed at the large shipping points of the Standard than prevailed at places where its competitors made most of their shipments. The Standard Oil Company located its refineries at points nearer the place of consumption, and so economized in shipping distance. Thus it transferred most of its business from Cleveland to Whiting, Indiana, in order to be nearer the Southern market and to the West, and began to supply the Eastern market from its refineries at Bayonne, New Jersey. By wise distribution of its refineries the Standard became largely independent of the changing freight rates that distressed those in-

the Standard Oil Company, and many of them further state that the Standard Oil Company has used its influence with the railways to maintain agreed tariff rates and to support the Interstate Commerce Act. (pp. 515–528.)

105

dependent refiners who shipped their oil long distances.[1] A less honorable advantage, it has been alleged, accrued to the Standard by the practice, among the railroads, of under-billing the weight of the contents of the tank-car. As to interstate shipments, this has been specifically denied by representatives of the Standard Oil Company; and the instances where such under-billing has occurred are explained as occasional errors.[2]

Immediately after the passage of the Interstate Commerce Act and the creation of the Interstate Commerce Commission the relative charges and advantages of tank and barrel shipments were brought in issue. Prior to 1888 it was universal to charge lower rates per one hundred pounds for oil in tanks than for oil in barrels; but in 1888 the Interstate Com-

[1] A vast amount of evidence bearing on this point is summarized in *Report of the Industrial Commission*, 1900, i., pp. 161–163.

[2] Evidence bearing on this point is digested in *Report of the Industrial Commission*, 1900, i., p. 165.

merce Commission ordered that the rates
on oil in tank-cars and in barrels should
be the same, the weight of the barrels
being included in the weight charged upon.
The railways complied generally with the
order of the Interstate Commerce Commission; but later, when the independent
refiner secured an order from the commission that the weight of barrels should
be disregarded in charging for shipments
of oil, the railways refused to comply with
this order or to pay the damages assessed
in reimbursement of the charge made for
the weight of the barrels.[1] As to the relative advantages of tank-cars and barrels,
and whether a relatively lower charge for
oil in tank-cars than for oil in barrels is
justifiable, there was much disagreement.
The tank-car, it appears, is always unloaded by the consignee and loaded by
the shipper, while the contrary is usually

[1] "A case raising this point is pending before the
United States courts."—*Report of the Industrial
Commission*, 1900, i., p. 788.

true with barrels. The barrel, it was urged, should not be carried free of charge because it is a merchantable article and its value is added to the price of the oil sold. On the other hand, the box-car in which the barrels are shipped can contain a return load, while the tank-cars must be returned empty.[1] The Standard is the largest shipper by tank-cars and owns most of the tank-cars in use. It gains not only such advantages as are given to shippers by tank-cars, but also the mileage of three-fourths of a cent per mile which is paid by the railways for the use of its cars.[2]

With nothing more exciting than an occasional case before the Interstate Commerce Commission regarding shipments by tank-car, the Standard Oil Trust continued

[1] This question is discussed by the Interstate Commerce Commission in the following cases: i., pp. 503, 722 ; ii., p. 389 ; iii., p. 186 ; iv., p. 228 ; v., pp. 193, 660.

[2] *Report of the Industrial Commission*, 1900, i., pp. 167–170.

from 1887 until 1892. Its growth and prosperity had been steady. The property of the various companies that entered the trust in 1882 was valued at $75,000,000. In 1892 the value was estimated at $121,-631,312; and fifty per cent. of this increase had come from profits invested and the remainder from additional capital subscribed.[1] The dividends meanwhile had risen from five and a quarter per cent. in 1882 to twelve per cent in 1891. During the ten years following 1882 there had been a gentle decrease in the price of refined oil and a slight decrease in the difference between the price of refined and the price of crude oil—a difference which measures the charge for refining.[2] The attitude of the Standard Oil Trust during these years was one of quiet dominance. It was now to meet an unexpected dif-

[1] Statement of Mr. S. C. T. Dodd, *Report of the Industrial Commission*, 1900, i., p. 799.
[2] *Industrial Combinations and Prices*, by J. W. Jenks, *Report of the Industrial Commission*, 1900, i., p. 52.

ficulty in the courts, which rendered necessary a complete change of organization.

1892–1903

In 1891 the State of Ohio, by its at-
torney-general, began action to oust the
Standard Oil Company of its corporate
rights, on the ground that it had abused its
corporate franchises in becoming a party
to an agreement against public policy. The
petition averred that in "violation of law
and in abuse of its corporate powers, and
in the exercise of privileges, rights, and
franchises not conferred upon it," the defendant company had become a party to
the trust agreements of 1882. "All the
owners and holders of its capital stock,
including all the officers and directors of
said defendant company, signed said agreements without attaching the corporate
name and seal." Prior to the dates of the
trust agreement aforesaid, the petition continued, the defendant's capital stock con-

110

sisted of thirty-five thousand shares. Upon the signing of said agreements thirty-four thousand nine hundred and ninety-three shares of said stock, belonging to the persons who signed the agreement, were transferred upon the defendant's books to the nine trustees appointed and named in the agreement, by virtue of which "the nine trustees have been, ever since the signing of said agreements, and still are, able to choose and have chosen annually such boards of directors of said defendant company as they (said nine trustees) have seen fit, and are able to and do control the action of the defendant in the conduct and management of its business."[1]

In answer to this petition the Standard Oil Company denied that it had become a party to either of the agreements in said petition set forth, or that it had at any time observed or carried out those agreements. "Said agreements," continued the

[1] "State *ex rel. v.* Standard Oil Company, 49 Ohio St.," pp. 138–155.

answer, "were agreements of individuals in their individual capacity and with reference to their individual property, and were not nor were they designed to be corporate agreements, and defendant denies that said agreements have illegally affected its corporate capacity or that defendant has permitted its corporate powers, business, and property to be exercised, conducted, and controlled in an illegal manner." [1]

By a demurrer to the defendant's plea the issue was squarely raised whether the act of all the stockholders, officers, and directors of a corporation may rightly be called the act of the corporation. "It seems to us," the plaintiff argued, "impossible to read the agreement and consider the proceedings which confessedly have taken place under it without reaching the conclusion that there has been a studious design and effort on the part of

[1] "State *ex rel. v.* Standard Oil Company, 49 Ohio St.," pp. 155–158.

the promoters of the trust scheme to obtain all the advantages of the actual presence and participation of the defendant corporation in the objects and purposes of the agreement without formally making it a party to it. But is substance to be sacrificed to shadow? Have we not shown sufficient actual corporate conduct to obviate the necessity for formal corporate action, such as the adoption of resolutions or the signing of a name?"[1]

The court adopted the argument of the plaintiff, and in its decision handed down March 2, 1892, based its rule on substantially the following reasons:

" A corporation, apart from the persons who compose it, is, by the fiction of the law, to be regarded as a legal entity only for convenience in the transaction of its business. When all or a majority of the stockholders' corporation do an act which affects the property and business of the company, and which, through the control

[1] " State *ex rel. v.* Standard Oil Company, 49 Ohio St.," p. 163.

their numbers give them over the selection and conduct of the corporate agencies, does affect the property and business of the company in the same manner as if it had been a formal resolution of its board of directors, and the act so done is *ultra vires* of the corporation and against public policy, the act should be regarded as the act of the corporation, and, to prevent the abuse of the corporate power, may be challenged by the State. The trust agreements in question are acts which must be regarded as the acts of the corporations, and, as such, *ultra vires;* and, tending as they do to the creation of a monopoly, to the control of prices as well as of production, these acts are also against public policy, and accordingly contrary to law."[1]

The place this case occupies in the law of corporations is of the first importance. A previous case, in which the Sugar Trust was defendant,[2] had decided that an agreement of associations to which the corporations were party was *ultra vires*. Further than declaring partnership of cor-

[1] "49 Ohio St.," pp. 176–189.
[2] "People *v.* North River Sugar Refining Company, 121 N. Y.," p. 582.

porations illegal, however, the law had not yet gone; and upon the question whether such combination was illegal, because in restraint of trade and opposed to public policy, the court had declined to express an opinion. In the instance of the Standard Oil Company the court made a bold advance: it not only forbade members of several corporations to combine as such and merge their interests in a trust, but it also declared such combination a restraint of trade, illegal, and quite opposed to public policy, and by the force of its decision put an end to the trust as a form of business combination.[1]

Accordingly, in 1892, the Standard Oil Trust was dissolved and the separate establishments and plants reorganized into twenty constituent companies. The trust certificates, when surrendered, were replaced by a proportion of the shares of each company, properly divided. By the

[1] S. C. T. Dodd, "The Present Legal Status of Trusts," 7 *Harvard Law Review*, p. 157.

form of transfer adopted the trustees placed in the hands of their attorney the amount of shares held by the trustees in the several companies of the trust, and authorized the attorney to secure from each of these companies transfer upon their corporate books of stock certificates for whole shares and scrip for fractional shares thereof. Although the trust was formally dissolved, the men who were the trustees hold a majority of the stock in all the different companies which composed the trust, so that they work together as harmoniously as before. The replacement of trust certificates by proportional shares of stock in the separate companies continued slowly and is not yet complete. Substantial unity of action among the several companies was not changed.[1]

[1] Precisely what may be called a "monopoly in restraint of trade" the courts have not clearly decided. Indefinite increase of business, the fixing of arbitrary prices, and the agreement not to trade with any one that trades with others than the covenantors have all been held not to be "monopoly"

The Standard Oil Company

Since the agreement between the Tidewater Pipe-Line Company and the National Transit Company, 1883, by which the Standard "alliance" had attained the dominant position in the transportation situation, there had been few attempts on the part of the independent producers to build pipe-lines. Under the impulse of the agreement among the producers and the Standard, in 1887, to restrict the production of oil, the Producers' Oil Company, Limited, had been organized and a pipe-line built from Titusville and Oil City to the new McDonald oil-field. But this

under the federal anti-trust act. On the other hand, American courts have held that the fact that "monopoly" has cheapened prices will not be considered, and that it makes no difference whether the monopoly be created by "contract" or "patent"; the people, they declare, ought not as a body to be employees and servants. A "monopoly" need not be "permanent" or "complete"; it may exist even if the article be susceptible of "indefinite production," and occurs when there is a "limitation" of "competition" and "production" with a view to "advance prices." (Cases are collected in 7 *Harvard Law Review*, pp. 348–355.)

was a local pipe-line, and was speedily absorbed by another company, the Producers' and Refiners' Oil Company, in which independent refiners as well as producers were interested. In 1890 occurred the first attempt on the part of the independent refiners to build to the seaboard a pipe-line which should afford them transportation facilities equal to those of the Standard. With this aim in view the United States Pipe-Line was projected.

The prime-mover and first president of this company was Mr. Lewis Emery, an independent refiner in Bradford, Pennsylvania. To avoid heavy transportation charges, he had determined in 1890 to build a pipe-line to the coast; and, pending the farther extension of his line, he had gone to the president of the Reading Railroad to secure a contract for transporting oil by that railroad from Williamsport, Pennsylvania. He was unable to make satisfactory terms, and accordingly determined to lay a pipe-line along the boundary of

New York and Pennsylvania to Hancock, New York, and to secure a contract with the New York, Ontario and Western Railroad for transporting oil to the Hudson, with a right to construct a pipe-line later along its tracks. This contract was secured, and straightway the task of getting right of way for the pipe-line was begun.

Immediately the usual obstacle appeared.[1] The opponents of the new company began to seek the right of way over the same route. They bought mortgages against pieces of land along the route, to induce the owners to give them another right of way. They bought strips of land crossing the projected route. The railroads also proved unsympathetic. When an attempt was made to lay the pipe-line under the Erie Railroad at Bradford, it was opposed by force, and later prevented by injunction from the courts. Another attempt to cross the Erie at Hancock met

[1] *Report of the Industrial Commission*, 1900, i., pp, 445, 486.

with similar fate. As a result, the pipe-line had to be constructed back seventy miles to the Susquehanna River, and built from Athens to Wilkesbarre. The crossing of every railroad brought on a legal contest, and before Wilkesbarre was reached $150,000 had been spent in litigation.[1]

These vexatious delays were not different in degree or kind from those met by any railroad or pipe-line in the securing of its right of way. In almost every case they were due to the desire of land-owners and speculators to extort from the constructing company a high price for what the company absolutely needed. The National Transit Company, no less than the United States Pipe-Line, had met these difficulties.[2] In the instance of the United States Pipe-Line Company the motive for

[1] Testimony of Mr. Emery, *Report of the Industrial Commission*, 1900, i., pp. 650–655.

[2] *Report of the Industrial Commission*, 1900, i., pp. 445, 486.

the opposition of the railroads was clearly the desire to preserve the great advantages in the oil traffic which their contract with the National Transit Company had secured them. The Standard Oil Company, it appears, was not engaged in these obstructionary tactics—for the very sufficient reason, indeed, that the projected pipe-line much more vitally concerned the interests of the railroads than it did those of the Standard.

For some time the pipe-line transported oil from Wilkesbarre by rail over the New Jersey Central Railroad. It then sought to continue its course to the seaboard. It crossed the Pennsylvania Railroad by purchasing an acre of land. When it reached the Delaware, Lackawanna and Western Railroad it bought a farm in Washington, New Jersey, over which the railroad crossed, hoping that it might lay a pipe-line under the culvert. One Saturday night it laid its pipes and stationed an armed force of fifty men to protect them. Next Monday two wrecking-cars of the railroad, with two hundred and fifty men, rode in from Hoboken, and attempted to oust the employees of the pipe-line company. Resistance was made, and, to compromise the matter, it was arranged that men on each side should be arrested in order to make a peaceable legal fight in the courts. But while these proceedings were going on a couple of locomotives were brought up by the railroad, and hot coals, hot water, and stones were thrown into the culvert. Finally the railroad employees were driven away, and the pipe-line employees secured rifles and held possession of the field for seven months. The lower courts decided in favor of the pipe-line, but after four years of litigation the Supreme Court of New Jersey decided that the pipe-line must be removed.

Eventually the United States Pipe-Line will build to Philadelphia. Meanwhile it transports its oil from Washington, New Jersey, fifty miles over the New Jersey

Central Railroad to New York,[1] at a rate much lower than the Standard has ever received for like distances. According to the contract between the railroad and the Pipe-Line Company, crude oil is carried fifty-two and one-half miles at the rate of $7.93 per tank-car, containing twenty tons; and the railroad returns the empty cars free. The contract is for one hundred years, and may be abrogated by the pipe-line upon five years' notice, the railroad having no right to abrogate it.[2]

Meantime the Standard Oil Company bought a large proportion of the stock of the Producers' Oil Company, with a view, as it would appear, to securing a controlling voice in its management; but it was so opposed in its ownership that it transferred its shares to a certain Mr. John J. Carter. Mr. Carter brought suit to be allowed to vote his stock, but, as the organization was a limited partnership, the courts upheld

[1] *Report of the Industrial Commission*, 1900 i., pp. 650–655.   [2] Ibid., pp. 513, 529.

the company in denying him admission.[1]
With the United States Pipe-Line Company the National Transit Company was
more successful.   It secured $383,000 out
of a total of $1,119,000 of stock, and, after
permission to attend the meetings of the
company and to vote the stock had been
refused by unaminous vote of the other
stockholders, the courts decided in favor
of the National Transit Company.   The
purchase of stock was made, says Mr.
Archbold, "with a view to having such
knowledge as we could have rightfully
through such ownership—as we should ac-
quire in the progress of the affair";[2] and this
information the National Transit Company
gets from its one director upon the board
of the United States Pipe-Line Company.[3]

To prevent the Standard Oil Company
from obtaining control of these independent organizations, the Pure Oil Company
was projected in June, 1895, to secure con-

[1] *Report of the Industrial Commission*, 1900, i.,
270, 577.   [2] Ibid., p. 577.   [3] Ibid., p. 656.

trol of the other independent companies.
In 1897 the Pure Oil Company was organized as a New Jersey corporation with
authorized capital stock of $1,000,000, of
which $377,000 has been paid in. The
business of the company has been marketing refined oil, especially in Germany, and
it has proposed to increase its capital to
$10,000,000.[1] In its structure this com-
pany is curiously like the former Standard
Oil Trust. The holders of sixty-six thousand shares in the company, being more
than a majority, vest the voting power of
such shares in fifteen persons for twenty
years; and it is agreed that one-half of all
shares hereafter subscribed shall similarly
be transferred to the trustees. The ownership of the shares may be transferred, but
purchasers have no rights other than those
provided by the trust agreement. The
trustees are to vote as a unit, to the full
number of the shares they hold, at the elec-

[1] *Report of the Industrial Commission*, 1900, i.,
p. 261.

tion of directors. One-third of the trustees retire annually, and their successors are elected by the general stockholders. By a vote of three-fifths of both classes of stockholders, on the redemption of the preferred shares at $110, the trust may be cancelled.[1] The formation of the voting trust, it was claimed, was made necessary by the attempt of the National Transit Company to secure control through the purchase of shares of the Producers' Oil Company and the United States Pipe-Line Company. In order to keep the control of the latter company in hands friendly to the independent interests, there was devised a voting-trust agreement, according to which the signers vested their interests in the stock in a certain Mr. A. D. Wood as trustee for five years from the 1st of April, 1893, unless sooner terminated by a vote of three-fourths of the stock so held in

[1] A copy of the trust agreement of the Pure Oil Company is given in *Report of the Industrial Commission*, 1900, i., pp. 466–470.

trust. Mr. Wood was allowed full power to elect officers, but was bound to vote for persons interested in the business as independent refiners.[1] It is the purpose of the Pure Oil Company, at the expiration of this trust agreement, to anticipate any attempt of the Standard Oil Company to control the company.

While the independent refiners have been seeking security in the trust form of organization, the Standard Oil Company has adopted the contrary policy. In 1892 the trust dissolved into its constituent companies, the former trustees holding a majority of the stock in each corporation and the holders of trust certificates exchanging them for the stock of the several companies in agreed proportion. By purely informal harmony, a unity of action among these corporations was maintained. A large quantity of trust certificates were still outstanding; and the dividends, when

[1] *Report of the Industrial Commission*, 1900, i., p. 110.

declared, were at a certain percentage upon these outstanding certificates and at a properly adjusted rate upon the capital stock of the different companies, so that the rate of dividends might be considered as if it were entirely on the trust certificates at their former full amount. In order to secure more complete unity and to provide for the claims of smaller holders of trust certificates, the Standard Oil Company was organized under the laws of New Jersey in 1899. This corporation, though practically a new organization, was in form a continuation of the old Standard Oil Company of New Jersey, with an amended charter and capital increased from $1,000,-000 to $110,000,000. This corporation was authorized to own the stock of any of the different corporations connected with the Standard Oil Company, and to buy from all parties who own such stock whenever they desired to sell.[1] "The new

[1] A copy of the charter of the company is given in *Report of the Industrial Commission*, 1900, i., p. 1228.

Standard Oil Company of New Jersey," said the Industrial Commission in 1900, "has recently been formed with the invention of transferring the stock of the different corporations into the stock of the new company, so that, when the transfer is finally made, one single corporation, the Standard Oil Company of New Jersey, will own outright the property now owned by the separate companies which are commonly known and mentioned together under the name of the Standard Oil Company. This combination at present has no formal unity. It has a practical unity as great as it will have probably after the complete change into the New Jersey company is affected."[1] Since 1900 about $97,-000,000 of the capital stock of this company has been used to purchase at par the stocks and properties of the other Standard companies, the capitalization of which was approximately $97,000,000, but whose

[1] *Report of the Industrial Commission*, 1900, i., p. 11.

129

good - will and earning power, as represented by the market value of the stock, aggregates $650,000,000.

Interesting as they are, the particular forms which the corporate organization of the Standard and of its competitors assume are the least important phase of their competition. The progress of both the Standard and the independent companies has been most marked in recent years in foreign countries. To place American oils in Eastern markets has required constant cheapening of production and transportation. An immense outlay for additional pipe-lines, more and larger steamers for ocean transportation, and the adoption of the tank-car and tank-wagon system of delivery have been made necessary, so that to-day crude oil is carried almost exclusively by pipe-lines, railroad transportation is confined to the products of crude oil, and the Standard has no arrangements apportioning to the railroads any share of the crude-oil traffic. At present it is in its methods of marketing, by which it meets competition at home and abroad, that the real interest lies.

Until 1895 the sale of crude oil by the producers had been on the exchange at Oil City. Throughout the eighties the market in the exchange had been wildly speculative, but, gradually, less and less oil came to be sold on exchange; and, finally, on January 23, 1895, the Seep Purchasing Agency of Oil City, on behalf of the Standard Oil Company, posted a notice that thereafter the prices paid by it to oil producers "will be as high as the market of the world will justify, but will not necessarily be the price bill on the exchange for certificate oil." The Seep Purchasing Agency purchases for the Standard Oil Company eighty per cent. of the crude oil produced in Pennsylvania and Ohio, and by its action it fixes the price of crude oil in the oil regions. "We have before us," says Mr. Archbold, "daily the best information obtainable from all the world's markets as to what the offerings are, and as to what it is possible to sell for; and we make from that the best possible consensus of prices, and that is our basis for arriving at the current price."[1] In the period from 1895 to the present, it may be added, the difference between the price of crude oil and the price of refined oil has remained almost constant,[2] which shows that this power of fixing the price of crude oil has not been abused, in spite of the fact that the Standard Oil Company during these years refined over eighty per cent. of the output of oil.[3]

By its control of the pipe-line systems the Standard Oil Company maintains its advantage over the independent refiners of the oil regions. The practice of the

[1] *Report of the Industrial Commission*, 1900, i., p. 571. See also pp. 142, 143.
[2] "Industrial Combinations and Prices," by J. W. Jenks, in *Report of the Industrial Commission*, 1900, i., p. 53.
[3] *Report of the Industrial Commission*, 1900, i., p. 560.

pipe-line companies is to receive all oil produced in the wells with which their pipes are connected, gauging the amount and recording the quantity received from each producer. The producer may then receive from the company at any time the value of his oil in store at the price for that day, or, instead, may receive pipe-line certificates which are negotiable in the open market. The company lays pipes without extra charge to new wells, though they be fifteen or twenty miles distant. In the proper management and extension of the pipe-lines, more than in any other branch of the business, is the necessity for large investments of capital apparent.[1] In the early days of the industry the absence of these facilities completely demoralized the business; and for the adequate management of the lines no company except the Standard has been ready and able to make the necessarily enormous

[1] *Report of the Industrial Commission*, i., pp. 285, 553, 799.

investment of capital. With their scant
resources the smaller companies were unable to respond to the slightest sudden
demand for new facilities. The superiority of the Standard Oil Company, in this
particular, was clearly shown in the sudden
development of the McDonald field in 1891.
In July of that year the output of the
McDonald field was three thousand barrels
daily. By the middle of August it had
reached fifteen thousand barrels. By the
first of September the Standard Oil Company, through its ally, the National Transit
Company, was able to handle twenty-six
thousand barrels a day; by the first of
October it could handle forty thousand
barrels a day; and when, in November,
the production of oil reached nearly eighty
thousand barrels per day, the capacity of
the pipe-lines had risen above that figure.
Iron tankage of the capacity of three
million barrels was erected during these
months, and fifty-three miles of pipe
laid in a territory of twelve square

134

miles.[1] Had the National Transit Company, with its $30,000,000 of invested capital, not been in control, it may be seriously doubted whether local enterprise could ever have effected so remarkable an extension of pipe-lines in so short a time.

Associated with its advantages in transportation is the advantage the Standard Oil Company has in distributing its refineries in strategic locations. Not only is a saving in transportation charges thus effected, but advantages accruing from cheaper land, labor, and fuel are also secured. To gain this economy, the Standard Oil Company spent millions in new plants near New York and Philadelphia.[2] It bought the entire output of the refineries in the newly discovered oil region in Colorado,[3] and secured control in 1898 of seventy-five per cent. of the refining business in Canada;[4] and for the same pur-

[1] *Report of the Industrial Commission*, 1900, i., pp. 471-475.   [2] Ibid., p. 649.
[3] Ibid., p. 384.   [4] Ibid., p. 673.

pose it has recently rebuilt refineries in Pennsylvania, in order to profit by the cheapened fuel.[1]

The vexed question of the effect of the Standard Oil combination on the price of refined oil will probably never be settled. Opponents of the Standard Oil Company declare that the Standard has not reduced the price of refined oil as compared with crude oil to any such degree as would be the case under open competition. The effect of the combination, they point out, is to be gauged only from the margin between the prices of refined and crude oil; and the reduction of this margin, though steady, is, in their opinion, by no means commensurate with the improvements in the processes of refining.[2] In reply, Mr. Archbold, of the Standard Oil Company, has

[1] *Report of the Industrial Commission*, 1900, i., p. 649.

[2] In the chart accompanying Professor Jenks's report on "Industrial Combinations and Prices," this margin is graphically shown. *Report of the Industrial Commission*, 1900, i.

declared that his company is unable permanently to exact excessive prices. Temporarily, it might have such power; but, if it used this power arbitrarily, it would provoke heavier competition. There is, he admits, a certain amount of monopolistic power, coming from the aggregation of capital itself, which keeps prices higher than they would be under severe competition; but at present this power and its effect upon prices are very slight, and the lessened cost of doing business on a large scale more than compensates in lowered prices for the slight monopolistic power of getting higher prices.[1] Perhaps the most significant criticism which the independent refiners pass upon the price which the Standard Oil Company gets for its oil is that the improved methods of utilizing by-products in recent years have made by-products as remunerative as the refined oil itself; and yet the margin of

[1] *Report of the Industrial Commission*, 1900, i., pp. 569, 570.

price between refined oil and crude oil during this period has only slightly decreased. The statement has frequently been made that the Standard has reduced its prices in the territory of its competitors, and maintained prices at more profitable rates at non-competitive points.[1] Such a practice, as an instance of ordinary business competition, is not extraordinary. A similar charge could be brought against most large businesses; and, as those who bring the charge seldom take into account the varying cost of transportation to markets of varying means of communication, small probative value can be attached to their bare statement of difference in price. Of more serious nature are the charges that the Standard Oil Company suborns the employees of its competitors to secure information as to their shipments and customers, and that

[1] A mass of evidence bearing on this point is digested in *Report of the Industrial Commission*, 1900, i., pp. 112–117.

it resorts to unfair tests and adulteration
of its oils and to the copying of brands
with the design to deceive purchasers. On
all these points the evidence is at best
vague and inconclusive. The officials of
the Standard Oil Company testify that it
is their practice to ask their salesmen to
keep their eyes open, and to inform the
company as to those from whom different
dealers are buying; but they flatly deny
the charge of suborning the employees of
their rivals, and very conclusively ex-
plain away the charge of fraud in the
copying of brands and in the tests and
adulteration of their products.[1] The en-
ergy of the Standard Oil Company, in
developing new departments of the industry, and its enterprise in undertaking
the production of all the chemicals and
materials incidental to the process of refining, has been recognized, even by independent refiners, as truly great, and

[1] *Report of the Industrial Commission*, 1900, i.,
pp. 118–127.

quite beyond what smaller competitors could have attempted.[1] The leading by-products are gasoline, naphtha, paraffine, lubricating oils, and vaseline products. In addition to these, fully two hundred other by-products are extracted and used for medical purposes and for aniline dyes. To utilize all these by-products requires the greatest specialization of methods, encouragement of invention, investment of capital, and extension of plant. A refinery of a capitalization of $500,000 cannot realize such economies.[2] The undoubtedly large profit accruing to the Standard Oil Company from the utilization of by-products is owing entirely to its superior mechanical efficiency and organization.

Aggregation of capital has brought to the Standard Oil Company its greatest advantage in the development of foreign

[1] Lewis Emery, *Report of the Industrial Commission*, 1900, i., p. 627.

[2] *Report of the Industrial Commission*, 1900, i., p. 570.

trade. In its contest on the Continent, and especially in Russia, with the great oil interests of the Rothschilds, of the Nobel Brothers, and of prominent English capitalists, its success has been entirely due to its great capitalization. Since 1871 the export of petroleum products has increased seven times, and of the present exports the Standard Oil Company ships ninety per cent.[1] In Russia the competition between the Standard and the Nobel Brothers is keen. The price of Russian crude oil is lower than that of American oil; and the Nobels are at present shipping it in tank steamers to India, China, and Japan. To meet this competition, the Standard Oil Company has established agencies all over the world, and has built bulk-tank-ships for transporting its product. With the exception of the trade in the Far East, where Russian competition is especially keen, the export price of oil

[1] *Report of the Industrial Commission*, 1900, i., p. 568,

has always been kept above the American price.[1]

The present position of the Standard Oil Company is one of abundant prosperity and power. It is opposed by a combination — the Pure Oil Company — which works in harmony with an independent seaboard pipe-line—the United States Pipe-Line — and with sixty - six independent refineries. The Standard controls ninety per cent. of the export trade and eighty per cent. of the domestic trade. By its control of the pipe-line situation it has become quite independent of the railroads. By its preponderant purchases of crude oil it has been able to steady and roughly direct the course of prices of petroleum. By its advantages in locating its refineries near their several markets and in utilizing by-products it has effected enormous economies in transportation and manufacture, and increased its dividend from twelve

[1] *Report of the Industrial Commission*, 1900, i., p. 791.

per cent. in 1892,[1] when the Standard Oil Trust was dissolved, to forty - eight per cent. in 1901. The power of the Standard Oil Company is tremendous, but it is only such power as naturally accrues to so large an aggregation of capital; and in the persistence with which competition against it has continued, in the quickness with which that competition increases when opportunity for profit under existing prices appears, and in the ever-present possibility of competition which meets the Standard Oil Company in the direction of every part of its policy, lie the safeguards against the abuse of this great power.

[1] *Report of the Industrial Commission*, 1900, i., p. 799.

THE END

Big Business
Economic Power in a Free Society
An Arno Press Collection

La Follette, Robert Marion, editor. **The Making of America:** Industry and Finance. 1905

Lilienthal, David E. **Big Business:** A New Era. 1952

Lippincott, Isaac. **A History of Manufactures in the Ohio Valley to the Year 1860.** 1914

Lloyd, Henry Demarest. **Lords of Industry.** 1910

McConnell, Donald. **Economic Virtues in the United States.** 1930

Mellon, Andrew W. **Taxation:** The People's Business. 1924

Meyer, Balthasar Henry. **Railway Legislation in the United States.** 1909

Mills, James D. **The Art of Money Making.** 1872

Montague, Gilbert Holland. **The Rise and Progress of the Standard Oil Company.** 1904

Mosely Industrial Commission. **Reports of the Delegates of the Mosely Industrial Commission to the United States of America, Oct.-Dec., 1902.** 1903

Orth, Samuel P., compiler. **Readings on the Relation of Government to Property and Industry.** 1915

Patten, Simon N[elson]. **The Economic Basis of Protection.** 1890

Peto, Sir S[amuel] Morton. **Resources and Prospects of America.** 1866

Ripley, William Z[ebina]. **Main Street and Wall Street.** 1929

Ripley, William Z[ebina]. **Railroads:** Rates and Regulation. 1912

Rockefeller, John D. **Random Reminiscences of Men and Events.** 1909

Seager, Henry R. and Charles A. Gulick, Jr. **Trust and Corporation Problems.** 1929

Taeusch, Carl F. **Policy and Ethics in Business.** 1931

Taylor, Albion Guilford. **Labor Policies of the National Association of Manufacturers.** 1928

Vanderlip, Frank A. **Business and Education.** 1907

Van Hise, Charles R. **Concentration and Control:** A Solution of the Trust Problem in the United States. 1912

The Wealthy Citizens of New York. 1973

White, Bouck. **The Book of Daniel Drew.** 1910

Wile, Frederic William, editor. **A Century of Industrial Progress.** 1928

Wilgus, Horace L. **A Study of the United States Steel Corporation in Its Industrial and Legal Aspects.** 1901

[Youmans, Edward L., compiler] **Herbert Spencer on the Americans.** 1883

Youngman, Anna. **The Economic Causes of Great Fortunes.** 1909